WITHDRAWN

Surviving Cold Weather

SIMPLY Survival

Greg Davenport's Books for the Wilderness

Gregory J. Davenport

MEMORIAL LIBRARY
500 N. DUNTON
ARLINGTON HEIGHTS, IL 60004

STACKPOLE
BOOKS

D0967330

0 11557 02635 1

11/04 LWD 6/04 1/2/07 W 3(1) 6/06 5(4)
9/09 Lad 2/08 - 6 (4)
1/11 Lad 11/10 8(4)

Copyright © 2002 by Gregory J. Davenport

For further information about Greg Davenport and Simply Survival, visit the website www.simplysurvival.com

Published by
STACKPOLE BOOKS
5067 Ritter Road
Mechanicsburg, PA 17055
www.stackpolebooks.com

All rights reserved, including the right to reproduce this book or portions thereof in any form or by any means, electronic or mechanical, including photocopying, recording, or by any information storage and retrieval system, without permission in writing from the publisher. All inquiries should be addressed to Stackpole Books, 5067 Ritter Road, Mechanicsburg, Pennsylvania 17055.

Printed in the United States

First Edition

10 9 8 7 6 5 4 3 2 1

Cover photograph by Steven A. Davenport
Cover design by Caroline Stover
Illustrations by Steven A. Davenport

Library of Congress Cataloging-in-Publication Data

Davenport, Gregory J.
    Surviving cold weather / Greg Davenport; [Illustrations by Steven A. Davenport].—1st ed.
       p. cm.—(Greg Davenport's books for the wilderness)
    Includes index.
    ISBN 0-8117-2635-5 (pbk.)
    1. Wilderness survival—Handbooks, manuals, etc. 2. Cold adaptation—Handbooks, manuals, etc. I. Title.

GV200.5 .D37 2003
613.6'9—dc21

                    2002008491

To Chuck and Glenda Davenport,
my parents

Contents

1

Introduction

Wilderness survival has many variables that dictate a person's success or failure. Each environment presents a myriad of unique challenges. Regardless of the environment, however, the same basic principles apply, from cold-weather to desert situations. Wilderness survival is a logical process, and using the following three-step approach to global wilderness survival will help you keep a clear head and proceed with meeting your needs—even under the most adverse conditions (for more details, read my book *Wilderness Survival*). This process is the key to survival in any environment. The only thing that differs is the order in which you meet your needs and the methods you use to meet them.

THE THREE-STEP APPROACH TO WILDERNESS SURVIVAL

1. Stop and recognize the situation for what it is.

   Often, when people realize they are in a legitimate survival situation, they panic and begin to wander aimlessly. This makes it harder for search-and-rescue teams to find them, and valuable time is lost that they could have spent meeting their needs. If you stop and deal with the situation—evaluating it and taking appropriate steps—your odds of survival are greatly increased.

2. Identify your five survival essentials, and prioritize them in order of importance for the environment you are in.

   1. Personal protection (clothing, shelter, fire).
   2. Signaling (man-made and improvised).
   3. Sustenance (identifying and procuring water and food).
   4. Travel (with and without a map and compass).
   5. Health (mental, traumatic, and environmental injuries).

   The exact order and methods of meeting these needs will depend on the environment you are in. Regardless of the order or method you

1

choose, these needs must be met. Various methods of meeting these needs in a cold-weather environment are covered throughout this text.

3. Improvise to meet your needs, using both man-made and natural resources.

Once you've identified your five survival essentials and prioritized them, you can begin to improvise to meet those needs. Sometimes the answer is straightforward, and sometimes it isn't. If you need some help deciding how to best meet one of your needs, use the five steps of improvising approach:

1. Determine your need.
2. Inventory your available man-made and natural materials.
3. Consider the different options of how you might meet your need.
4. Pick the one that best uses your time, energy, and materials.
5. Proceed with the plan, ensuring that the final product is safe and durable.

Being able to improvise is the key to a comfortable wilderness visit versus an ordeal that pushes the limits of mortality. Consider what natural materials might be available and how, together with man-made resources, they might be used to meet your five survival essentials. The only limiting factor to improvising is your imagination!

Greg Davenport's three-step approach to global survival.

2

Snow and Ice Climates

SNOW CLIMATES

The interior continental areas of the two great landmasses of North America and Eurasia that lie between 35 and 70 degrees north latitude constitute the snow climates. The pole side usually meets with the tundra climate, and the southern side with a temperate forest. Vegetation is similar to that found in the temperate climates. The inland animals are migratory yet obtainable. Most shorelines are scraped free of vegetation and animals by winter ice. The larger game animals, such as caribou, reindeer, goats, and musk oxen migrate in these climates. Small animals, such as snowshoe hares, mice, lemmings, and ground squirrels, are prominent. Many birds breed in snow climates. There are two basic kinds of snow climates: continental subarctic and humid continental.

CONTINENTAL SUBARCTIC CLIMATES

These are regions of vast extremes. Temperatures can have large swings, from –100 degrees F to 110 degrees F, and may fluctuate up to 50 degrees in several hours. These climates are most often seen in Alaska to Labrador and Scandinavia to Siberia. They are cold, snowy forest climates most of the year, with short summers. Winter is the dominant season.

HUMID CONTINENTAL CLIMATES

These regions are generally located between 35 and 60 degrees north latitude, in the central and eastern parts of continents of the middle latitudes. Seasonal contrasts are strong, and the weather is highly variable. In North America, this climate extends from New England westward beyond the Great Lakes region, into the Great Plains and the prairie provinces of Canada.

Summers are cooler and shorter than in other temperate zones. A high percentage of precipitation is snow.

   In both of these types of snow climates, there are seasonal extremes of daylight and darkness. Long nights and minimal sun exposure are common and present a problem for a survivor.

ICE CLIMATES

The terrain of an ice climate varies greatly. Most of the landmass is composed of tundra. In its true form, the tundra is treeless. Vast, rugged mountain ranges are found in the area and rise several thousand feet above the surrounding areas. Steep terrain, snow and ice fields, glaciers, and very high wind conditions make this a very desolate place. Continental glaciers, such as the ice caps covering Greenland and the Antarctic continent, are large expanses of wind-swept ice moving slowly toward the sea. Animal life is poor in species but rich in numbers. Commonly, large animals, birds, and fish can be found. In the Antarctic, however, animals are virtually nonexistent. Most common are seals and penguins, along with seabirds. There are three basic kinds of ice climates: marine subarctic, tundra, and ice cap.

MARINE SUBARCTIC CLIMATE

This climate is found between 50 and 60 degrees north latitude and 45 and 60 degrees south latitude on the windward coasts, on islands, and over wide expanses of ocean in the Bering Sea and North Atlantic, touching points of Greenland, Iceland, and Norway. In the Southern Hemisphere, the climate is found on small landmasses. These regions typically have persistent cloudy skies, strong winds, and high rainfall.

TUNDRA CLIMATE

This climate is found north of 55 degrees north latitude and south of 50 degrees south latitude. The average temperature is below 50 degrees F. Proximity to the ocean and persistent cloud cover keep summer air temperatures down, despite abundant solar energy at this latitude near the summer solstice. There are several types of tundra.

Shrub tundra
Shrubs, herbs, and mosses occur in this zone.

Wooded tundra

Subarctic wooded areas include a variety of tree species.

Bogs

Bogs are characterized by large peat moss mounds.

ICE CAP CLIMATE

There are three vast regions of ice on the earth: Greenland, the Antarctic continental ice caps, and the larger area of floating sea ice in the Arctic Ocean.

3

Gear

When traveling into a cold-weather environment, the type of gear you carry can either help or hamper your efforts. Take the time to choose tools that will make your travel and stay more comfortable.

ICE AX

An ice ax can be used as an anchor for climbing, as a self-belay, to help you self-arrest when sliding down a snow slope (glissading), and to help steady you while climbing by providing a third point of contact. The proper size of an ice ax depends on your body size and the ax's intended use. To size an ice ax, hold its head in one hand, with your fingers draped down the side of the shaft. While standing up straight, let your arm hang free so that the ice ax shaft is pointing toward the ground. From this position, use the following guidelines:

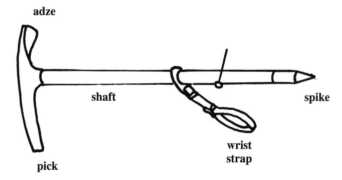

Ice ax

For basic climbing (general use)
The ax tip should be just shy of touching the ground.

For intermediate climbing (high-angle use)
The ax tip should be 2 to 4 inches (5 to 10 centimeters) shy of the ground.

For snowshoeing
The ax tip should extend 2 to 4 inches (5 to 10 centimeters) beyond the ground.

SNOW SHOVEL

A snow shovel can be used to evaluate avalanche hazards, dig out an avalanche victim, or help build a snow shelter. The ideal snow shovel is small and light enough to carry, yet big and strong enough to perform the needed task. A 20- to 24-inch-long aluminum shovel that has a removable D-shaped handle and one-foot-square blade is a good all-purpose design. A snow or ice saw is often used with a snow shovel, especially when snow blocks are needed for shelter walls. In a pinch, I have used my snowshoes to shovel snow. Should you do this, however, be careful not to break a snowshoe!

MOUNTAINEERING POLES

Mountaineering poles help you maintain your balance when carrying a heavy pack and assist you in getting up should you fall. Unlike ski poles, most mountaineering poles have adjustable telescoping features that allow them to do multiple tasks, adjusting for uphill, downhill, and traversing pole lengths. In addition, when not in use, they can collapse down for easy storage. When using a pole, adjust its length so that when your elbow is bent, your forearm is slightly less than perpendicular to your body, with the hand higher than the elbow. If you are evaluating this length in a store, place the handle side down and grasp the pole below its basket, since the length is based on the pointed tip being inserted into the snow up to the basket.

PROBE

A probe is an essential item when traveling into terrain where the chance for avalanche conditions is present. Probes should be lightweight, strong, and quickly assembled. Most probes run from 8 to 10 feet and can be broken down into 16- to 18-inch lengths for ease of carrying. Aluminum is the most common material, as it is lightweight and inexpensive. In a pinch, a mountaineering pole can be used.

AVALANCHE TRANSCEIVER

An avalanche transceiver is an electronic device that, when used properly, helps searchers find a victim who has been buried in an avalanche. When traveling in avalanche hazard areas, each member of the team should carry a transceiver, or beacon. The newer transceivers are digital with dual antennas, digital and analog, which has made them far more efficient. The Barryvox digital transceiver (RED 457) has an integrated microprocessor, digital technology, a simple pushbutton menu, and an easy-to-follow digital display that displays the direction and distance to your subject.

PIEPS avalanche transceiver

AVALUNG

The AvaLung is an innovative idea that should become standard gear for anyone traveling into avalanche country. It is a filtration system designed to help an avalanche victim breathe by drawing air directly from the snowpack through a mouthpiece attached to the apparatus. Exhaled carbon dioxide is directed out an exhaust tube, ensuring that you receive a fresh air supply and preventing the formation of an oxygen-depriving ice layer in front of your face. To be effective, the mouthpiece must be quickly inserted into your mouth before debris restricts your movement.

CLINOMETER

A clinometer helps you determine avalanche hazards by measuring the slope of a hillside. Avalanches most often occur on slopes of 30 to 45 degrees, but they sometimes start on slopes as gentle as 25 degrees or as steep as 60 degrees. Recognizing a slope angle is key to identifying a slope's avalanche potential. The clinometer is simply a protractor with a plumb bob attached. While the plumb bob is hanging free, you hold the base parallel to the

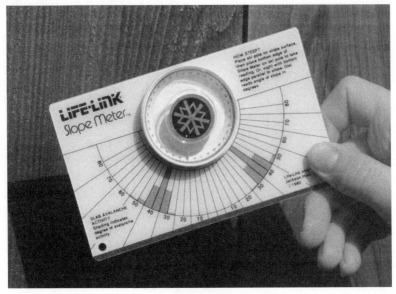

Clinometer

hillside. The number where the plumb bob line crosses the protractor is your slope angle.

ALTIMETER

A digital altimeter can provide information about your elevation that, when used along with a map and the terrain, can help you pinpoint your location. Since an altimeter reading is based on air pressure, like a barometer, it is affected by changes in weather. With this in mind, you'll need to set its elevation from a known point when you start, and again on a regular basis as you reach new known points.

SNOWSHOES

Snowshoes are an outstanding aid when traveling on snow and are especially helpful when carrying a pack. They make travel easier by dispersing your weight over a greater surface area, which in turn eliminates the posthole effect caused by snowshoeless feet. Snowshoes are superior to cross-country skis in snow-covered areas that also have brush or rock obstacles, and they are easier to use than skis for those who are inexperienced. Modern snowshoes are made of an oval-shaped, lightweight, tubular frame that supports a durable decking material. Most bindings are easy to attach to your boots and come with cramponlike metal plates at the toes and heels to aid in traction. The type of snowshoes you'll need depends on their intended use and your weight. Smaller-style snowshoes allow greater maneuverability, whereas larger ones provide greater flotation.

SNOWSHOE DESIGNS

There are four basic snowshoe designs: Yukon, Beavertail, Bearpaw, and Western.

Yukon

Yukon, or trail, snowshoes are large, measuring on average 40 to 60 inches long and 10 inches wide, with a 6- to 8-inch toe turnup. They are good shoes for open terrain where deep powder is present. Although you can travel up and down steep slopes, you will have to traverse them. These shoes are often made from wood and have neoprene laced decking.

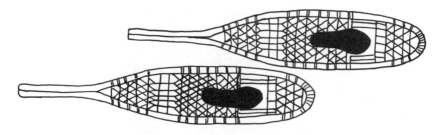

Yukon snowshoes

Beavertail

The Beavertail design ranges in size from 9 by 40 inches to 20 by 44 inches. The most popular size appears to be the 12-by-34-inch. These shoes are generally flat, with a large, oval body that supports a long tail. They are decent shoes for kick-stepping but do not perform well when traversing a hill. These shoes are often made from wood and have neoprene laced decking.

Bearpaw

The Bearpaw design ranges in size from 12 by 24 inches to 19 by 26 inches. The most popular size appears to be the 12-by-28-inch. These flat-toed, short, and wide snowshoes support no tail and are good shoes for

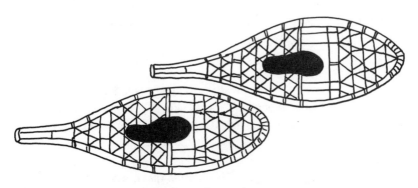

Beavertail snowshoes

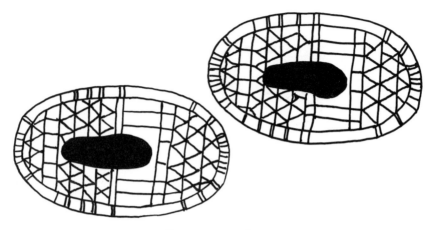

Bearpaw snowshoes

kick-stepping but not for open terrain. These shoes are often made from wood and have neoprene laced decking.

Western

The Western design ranges in size from 8 by 22 inches to 9 by 38 inches. These shoes have an aluminum frame and most often use a plastic decking. The tubular aluminum is very strong and light, and the solid plastic decking provides superior flotation compared with lace decking. The Western-style mountaineering snowshoe is a great all-purpose design, which allows travel in all terrains and performs well when ascending or descending slopes.

CHOOSING SNOWSHOES

Atlas Snow-Shoe Company provides the FACT (Flotation, Articulation, Comfort, and Traction) acronym for selecting Western-style snowshoes. These are the basic factors you should consider when purchasing snowshoes.

Flotation

A snowshoe's surface area provides flotation that keeps you from sinking through the snow's surface. Pick the smallest snowshoes that will support your weight plus the weight of your backpack and gear. As a general rule, however, choose larger snowshoes for dry snow and smaller ones for snow that is wet and dense.

Articulation
Articulation refers to how well snowshoe bindings allow your foot to move once attached. Under ideal circumstances, a binding will limit stepping rotation, allow the ankle freedom of rotation, and minimize heel twist.

Stepping rotation
Snowshoes should allow your feet to bend—from front to back—in a motion similar to walking. At the same time, the snowshoes' tips should not hit your shins and the shoes should not drag.

Ankle rotation
A snowshoe binding should support the foot while still allowing the ankle to naturally rotate from side to side. To accomplish this, bindings need to flex enough to allow the ankle to freely rotate from side to side, keeping it in a neutral position regardless of the terrain.

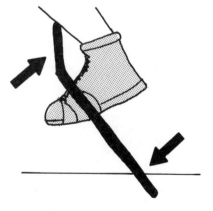

Correct stepping rotation   *Incorrect stepping rotation*

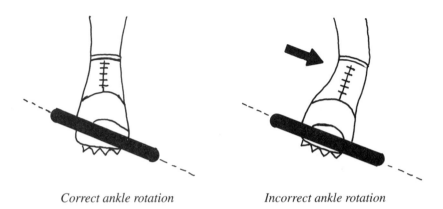

Correct ankle rotation   *Incorrect ankle rotation*

Heel support

A snowshoe's binding should allow for stepping rotation and ankle rotation, while keeping your foot centered—from side to side—regardless of the terrain.

Comfort

A comfortable binding, like a comfortable boot, should be made for the specific foot, not have any pressure points when snugly attached to the arch and ball of the foot, and be easy to put on and take off.

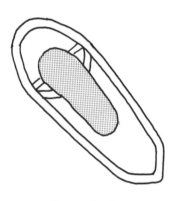
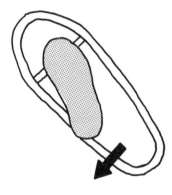

Correct heel support   *Incorrect heel support*

Traction

Unless you intend to snowshoe on perfectly level ground, you'll need snow-shoes that can provide traction when ascending, descending, or traversing a slope. To provide this traction, your snowshoes should have cleats, or crampons, located at the toes, heels, and along the sides.

IMPROVISING SNOWSHOES

In a crisis, snowshoes can be improvised from boughs. Use boughs from a tree on which the smaller branches and needles are thick and abundant, such as fir. Cut five to ten boughs that are 4 to 5 feet long each, lash the bases of all the branches together, and loosely tie them around their mid-point. Secure the bough snowshoes to your feet by tying a line around the toe of your boot and the forward third of the boughs.

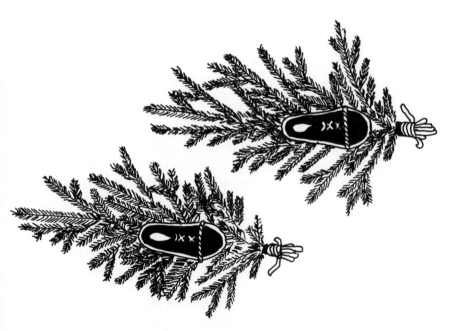

Snowshoes made from boughs

CRAMPONS

Crampons are normally made from extremely strong yet lightweight steel. The common twelve-point crampon supports ten side points (five on each side) and two forward-slanting points located at the toe. Consider the angle of the crampons' first two rows and whether the crampons are rigid or hinged when deciding what type to use.

For basic flat-footing and general use in climbing

Use hinged crampons with straight points, the first row pointing forward and subsequent rows down.

For steep slopes, where front-pointing

Use rigid crampons with the first row slightly dropped down and the second row angled toward the toe of the boot.

CROSS-COUNTRY SKIS

Nordic and mountaineering skis are good tools for snow travel but may not be the best option when carrying heavy backpacks or in a densely forested area. These skis use boot bindings that attach to your toes but leave the heels free. Mountaineering skis are slightly wider and heavier than the Nordic style and use bindings that leave the heels free for uphill travel but allow you to secure them when going downhill. If you intend to use your skis to travel uphill, you'll need climbing skins. These skins are attached to the bottom of the skis, providing the traction needed for uphill travel. An advanced cross-country skier can go almost anywhere, using skins to conquer uphill challenges and telemarking to descend steeper slopes.

SELECTING CROSS-COUNTRY SKIS,
BOOT, BINDINGS, AND POLES

If you intend to travel off-trail, purchase gear that is rated for touring to backcountry use. Cross-country skis allow you to move forward through a kicking and gliding process. While one foot is gliding, with only the toe and heel of the ski making firm contact with the snow, the other ski is kicking; the ski's center has traction and is making firm contact with the snow while moving backward and propelling you forward. If a ski is too firm in the center, you will have a great glide, but it will also require more work to propel you forward. These skis are best left to the pros. If a ski is too soft in the center, you will have less glide, but it will be easier to propel you forward. Some skis require wax, and others are waxless. Both styles, however, work on the same principle: They are slick at the ends and sticky at the center. On waxless skis, the front and back have little or no pattern, and the center has a tread pattern. If the skis require wax, the ends are waxed with a glide wax and the center with a sticky kick wax. Unless you are an advanced skier, I'd advise using waxless skis. They are easy to use and require little maintenance. You'll never have to worry about whether you have applied the right wax. A waxless ski, however, is slower than one that uses wax. Nevertheless, it is very versatile, allowing you to use it for a multitude of conditions, excluding ice travel. For backcountry skiing, use skis that are heavier and wider; when on groomed trails, use skis that are light and narrow. To select a ski that will optimize your abilities, you should consider your weight, height, and cross-country skiing ability.

Weight and ability

To determine the appropriate ski for your weight, hold the skis upright so that their bases are touching. There will be a gap in the center, caused by the skis' camber, or slight arching. As a basic rule of thumb, while holding these skis in this position, you should be able to squeeze the camber completely together using both hands. If you can't, the skis are probably too stiff and should be left for the advanced skier; if you can do it with one hand, they are probably too soft.

Height and ski length

For general use, when you hold the ski perpendicular to the ground and raise an arm over your head, it should reach your wrist. For backcountry use, however, select a ski that reaches to about the top of your head. The shorter ski will provide greater ease of turning and maneuverability between obstacles.

BOOTS AND BINDINGS

Be sure to buy boots designed for skiing and not skating. The boots need to have toe bars for binding attachment. Buy the boots first, and then select the bindings that will work with them. Most bindings are either step-in or

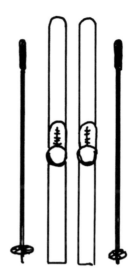

Cross-country skis, boots, and poles

manual styles. To use a step-in binding, you simply insert the toe of your boot into the binding's forward bar, and press down until it snaps into place. A manual binding requires you to secure a latch over the top of the boot's toe bar. Bindings should be mounted by a professional.

POLES

Your poles should have round baskets at the bottom. For general use, they should be somewhere between armpit and shoulder height. If touring, longer poles are better, but when in treed, mountainous terrain, shorter poles will serve you better. Expandable poles are ideal, since they allow you to change their length as needed for ascents and descents.

SLED

A sled allows you to carry more gear than just what fits into your pack and is a great option for long trips. Most commercial sleds come with a cover, waist harness, and support poles that connect the sled to your harness. You can make a similar item by attaching a child's sled to your pack or waist harness with rope. The benefit of the commercial sled is its rigid poles, which help you control it when traversing or going downhill. You might fashion such support poles by attaching lengths of thick PVC pipe to the sled and your pack or belt.

BACKPACK

There are two basic pack designs used by backcountry travelers: internal- and external-frame packs.

EXTERNAL-FRAME BACKPACK

The external-frame pack uses a frame that holds the pack away from your back. This is an advantage when traveling in hot weather, but it also makes the pack prone to sudden shifts that can occur without warning and disrupt your balance. An external-frame pack is best when used in extremely hot weather (during nontechnical travel) and when trail hiking.

John Glenn wearing an external-frame pack

INTERNAL-FRAME BACKPACK
In a snow and ice environment, an internal-frame pack is preferable. The internal frame's shape allows the pack to lie directly on your back, which allows for better balance as you travel.

The size of the pack you'll need depends on its use. For overnight trips, 3,000 to 5,000 cubic inches are appropriate, whereas for long trips, you'll need at least 5,000 or more cubic inches. When selecting a pack, make sure it fits your back's length and contour, has strong webbing, and provides thick shoulder and waist padding.

To make an improvised backpack, start by finding a forked branch (sapling or bough), and cut it 1 foot below the fork and 3 feet above. Trim off excess twigs, cut notches about 1 inch from each of the three ends, and tie rope or line around the notches of the two forked branches. Bring the

Dawn Sexton wearing an internal-frame pack

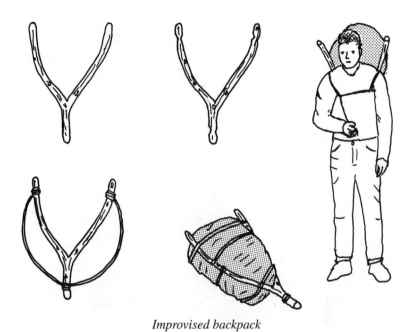

Improvised backpack

two lines down and tie them to the notch on the single end of the sapling to establish the pack's shoulder straps. Make sure the gap between the line and branch is wide enough for your shoulders to fit within, not too tight or too loose. Place your gear inside a waterproof bag, and attach it to the forked branch. To carry this pack, I'd advise creating a chest strap that runs through the shoulder straps at armpit height. This line should be long enough that you can hold its free end in your hand, allowing you to control the amount of pressure exerted by the pack on your armpits and shoulders.

CAMELBAK

The CamelBak was a great innovation that not only insures you'll stay hydrated but also creates a method to carry more emergency gear. I have several sizes, all of which allow me to carry 100 ounces of water and have a drinking nozzle located over the shoulder strap allowing easy access. When in camp, I always have it on. When on the trail I place it securely

Dawn-Marie Davenport's MULE CamelBak holds 3 quarts of water.

on top of my large pack with the water bladder's hose draped over my pack's shoulder strap. By doing this, I continue to have easy access to my water and can quickly get into my emergency gear when I stop. The HAWG can carry 1203 cubic inches (1020 in the cargo pocket) and weighs 1.9 pounds empty and approximately 8.2 pounds when its 100-ounce water reservoir is filled. It measures 9 x 7 x 19 inches. The HAWG CamelBak costs approximately $100.

SLEEPING BAG

There are many types of sleeping bags available, and the type used varies greatly among individuals. There are several basic guidelines you should use when selecting a bag. The ideal bag should be compressible, have an insulated hood, and be lightweight but still keep you warm. Most manufacturers rate their bags as summer, three-season, or winter expedition use and provide a minimum temperature at which the bag will keep you warm. This gross rating is used as a guide and should help you select the bag that best meets your needs. Sleeping bag covers are useful for keeping your bag clean and add an extra layer of insulating air. How well the bag will keep you warm depends on the design, amount and type of insulation and loft, and method of construction.

DESIGN

Without question, the hooded, tapered mummy style is the bag of choice for snow and ice camping. The hood should tighten around your face, leaving a hole big enough for you to breathe through. The foot of the bag should be somewhat circular and well insulated. Side zippers need good, insulated baffles behind them.

INSULATION

Sleeping bags are filled with either down or a synthetic material.

Down

Down is very lightweight, effective, and compressible. A down bag is rated by its fill power in cubic inches per ounce. A rating of 550 is standard, with values increasing in excess of 800. The higher ratings provide greater loft, meaning a warmer bag. The greatest downfall to this insulation is its inability to maintain its loft and insulating value when wet. In addition, it is very expensive.

Synthetic insulation

Synthetic materials provide a good alternative to down. Their greatest strength is their ability to maintain most of their loft and insulation when wet, along with their ability to dry relatively quickly. On the flip side, syn-

offset quilt   **slant tube**   **square box**

Sleeping bag construction designs

thetic insulation is heavier and doesn't compress as well as down. Although cheaper than down, it tends to lose its loft quicker with long-term use. Lite Loft and Polarguard are two great examples of synthetic insulations.

METHOD OF CONSTRUCTION
Insulation material is normally contained in baffles, which are tubes created within the bag. There are three basic construction designs for sleeping bags: slant tube, offset quilt, and square box. Each design has its benefits, and the type you should choose depends on many factors, including weight, temperature rating, and compressibility.

IMPROVISING A BAG
Understanding the basic bag design is the key to improvising a bag in a time of crisis. I once made a bag using ripstop parachute material, dry leaves, and moss.

SLEEPING PAD

A sleeping pad is essential for insulating you from the cold, moist ground. Most commercial pads are closed-cell or open-cell foam, or a combination of the two. Each style has its pros and cons.

CLOSED-CELL FOAM
These types of pads provide excellent insulation and durability but are bulky to carry. They may or may not have an outer nylon shell covering.

OPEN-CELL FOAM
These pads are often self-inflating, using a high-flow inflation valve. Their ability to compress and rebound makes them ideal when space is a concern. Open-cell foam pads are usually covered with a durable, low-slip polyester fabric.

IMPROVISING A PAD
If you don't have a pad, you can improvise one using boughs, moss, leaves, or similar dry materials. Make a mound that is 18 inches high and large enough to protect your whole body from the ground.

KNIVES

I often carry a folding pocketknife for the majority of my cutting work and a larger, fixed-blade knife for the bigger projects. I consider the pocketknife one of my most important tools, and thus its design is extremely important to me. The weakest part of a folding-blade knife is its lock—the part that keeps the blade open and prevents it from closing on your fingers.

This Benchmade knife uses a D2 steel, G10 handle, and patented axis lock, setting the standard for the folding-blade knife.

Busse Combat knives are straightforward knives made of Infi steel, setting the standard for the fixed-blade knife.

A good lock will secure the blade tightly to the handle when it is open. I prefer a blade length of 3 inches.

For the majority of my big projects, such as cutting down 2-inch-diameter dead trees or prepping the larger stages of my firewood, I use a large fixed-blade knife. A simple blade is all you will need. Avoid knives that have multiple modifications to the blade that supposedly allow you to do the unimaginable; it's just a bunch of marketing hype. I prefer a 7- to 9-inch knife blade, with the total length measuring around 15 to 17 inches.

The SCOLD acronym—(Sharp, Clean, Oiled, Lanyard, and Dry)—can help you remember the proper care and use of your knives.

SHARP

A sharp knife is easier to control and use, decreasing the chance for injury. Two methods of sharpening a knife—the push-and-pull and the circular technique—are outlined below, followed by general guidelines for obtaining a proper angle for your knife blade.

Push-and-pull technique

In a slicing fashion, repeatedly push and pull the knife's blade across a flat sharpening stone (if a commercial sharpening stone isn't available, use a flat, gray sandstone). For best results, start with the base of the blade on the long edge of the stone, and pull it across the length of the stone so that when you're done, its tip has reached the center of the stone. To obtain an even angle, push the other side of the blade across the stone in the same manner. Each side should be done the same number of times.

Circular technique
In a circular fashion, repeatedly move the knife blade across a circular sharpening stone or gray sandstone. Starting with the base of the blade at the edge of the stone, move the knife in a circular pattern across the stone. To obtain an even angle, turn the blade over and do the same on the other side. Each side should be done the same number of times.

Obtaining a proper angle
To establish the best sharpening angle, lay the knife blade flat onto the sharpening stone, and then raise the back of the blade up until the distance between it and the stone is equal to the thickness of the blade's back side.

Clean
Grit and dirt that get into the folding joint can destroy the joint and cause it to freeze closed or open, or even break. Dirt can also be harmful to the blade's steel and can lead to its deterioration. To clean a knife, use a rag, and wipe it from the backside of the knife to avoid cutting yourself. Never run the knife across your pants or shirt, since that will transfer the dirt into the pores of your clothing, and you might even cut your clothes or yourself.

OILED
Keeping the blade and joint of your knife oiled will help protect the joint and steel and decrease the chances of rust.

LANYARD
Before even thinking of using this knife, make sure you have it attached by a lanyard to your body. To determine the lanyard's proper length, hold the knife in your hand and fully extend your arm over your head, then add 6 more inches. This length allows you full use of the knife and decreases the risk of cuts due to a lanyard that is too short.

DRY

Keeping your knife dry is an important part of preventing rust, which can ruin the blade and its joint.

A knife has many uses and is probably one of the most versatile tools a survivor can carry. The potential for injury when using a knife is high, however, and you should take every precaution to reduce this risk, always cutting away from yourself and maintaining a sharp knife.

AX

An ax is a must when traveling into cold-weather environments. It can be used to fell a tree, cut poles, or split wood. Should a large fire be required, the ax enables you to obtain the larger dead wood necessary to sustain a fire. Rhythm, rather than brute force, is the key to properly using an ax. The last thing you want is a broken handle caused by a misguided forceful swing. The weight of a properly aimed ax is all that is required to get the job done.

FELLING TREES

If possible, always fell the tree in the direction of its naturally occurring lean. For safety, make sure to clear all debris and obstacles from the area within the scope of your swing. Make the first cut—a wedge—on the tree's downward-leaning side and as close to the ground as safely possible. The second cut should be on the opposite side, and just slightly higher than the first. *Caution:* Since trees often kick back at the last minute, make sure you have a clear escape route established. When cutting the tree's limbs, start at the bottom, and always stand on the side of the tree that is opposite of the side you are working on.

CUTTING POLES

When cutting poles hold the wood in your left hand and let it rest on top of and perpendicular to a downed log. With the ax in your right hand, strike the pole in a controlled downward motion, as illustrated. *Note:* Reverse this if you are left-handed. Not only does this technique help prevent physical injury, it also decreases the chances of damaging your ax. If you need to cut a pole in half and don't have an ax or a large knife, you can either burn it in half or use a small knife to cut notches around it until it easily snaps into separate pieces.

Felling a tree

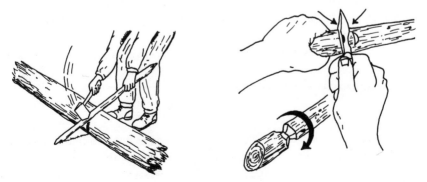

Cutting poles

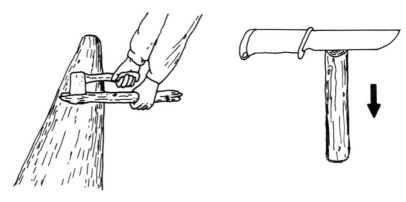

Splitting wood

SPLITTING POLES

When splitting a pole, hold it firmly in your left hand while, at the same time, holding the ax in your right hand. The pole and ax should be parallel to one another and the sharp side of the ax head should be on top and at the far end of the pole. Swing both the pole and the ax together, striking them on top of a downed log that is perpendicular to the pole and ax. If you are using a knife to split a pole, do not swing the knife down onto the pole. Instead, place the sharp side of the blade on top of the pole's cut end, and use a pounding stick to drive the knife into the wood, eventually splitting it.

A sharp ax is easier to use, thus decreasing the chances of injury. A file is often used to sharpen an ax. To do this, work the file from one end of the cutting edge to the other, using a controlled motion. Do this an equal number of times on each side. To help prevent accidental injury, file away from—not toward—the cutting edge. Once the edge is sharp, use a honing stone to smooth out any roughness.

SAWS

The Sven Saw and Pocket Chain Saw are two great items to consider taking into cold climates. Although I wouldn't consider them a replacement for the ax, both will help break down bigger sections of wood into a more workable size.

A Sven Saw is a useful tool for cutting large pieces of wood into shorter sections.

SVEN SAW
The lightweight Sven Saw is made from an aluminum handle and 21-inch steel blade that folds inside the handle for easy storage. When open, the saw forms a triangle measuring 24 x 20 x 14 inches; when closed, it measures 24 x 1½ x ½ inches. The saw weighs 16 ounces and costs around $22.

POCKET CHAIN SAW
The 31-inch heat-treated steel Pocket Chain Saw weighs only 6.2 ounces when stored inside a small 2¾ x ⅞ inch tin can. The saw has 140 bidirectional cutting teeth that will cut wood just like a chain saw; the manufacturer claims it can cut a 3-inch tree limb in less than 10 seconds. The kit comes with two small metal rings and plastic handles. The rings attach to the ends of the saw blade, and the handles slide into the rings, providing a grip that makes cutting easier. In order to save space, however, I don't carry the handles and simply insert two sturdy branches, about 6 x 1 inch, into the metal rings. The Pocket Chain Saw costs around $20.

The Pocket Chain Saw is an excellent small and compact tool for cutting wood into shorter sections.

BACKPACKING STOVE

When selecting a backpacking stove, you should consider its weight; the altitude and temperatures of where you are going; the stove's ease of operation, even in cold, wet, or windy conditions; and fuel availability. The two basic styles are canister and liquid fuel. Canister designs use butane, propane, or isobutane cartridges as their fuel source. The most common types of liquid fuels used are white gas and kerosene.

BUTANE OR PROPANE

A canister allows for a no-spill fuel that is ready for immediate maximum output. Butane and propane canisters are available throughout the United States and most of the world. I like these types of stoves due to their ease of use and unmatched performance. Some versions do not perform well in temperatures below freezing, however, and disposal of the used canisters can be a problem.

WHITE GAS

White gas has a high heat output and is highly available in the United States. Although the fuel quickly evaporates, it is highly flammable if spilled. The stove often does not require priming in order to start.

KEROSENE

Kerosene gas has a high heat output and is available throughout the world. Unlike white gas, when spilled, this fuel evaporates slowly and will not easily ignite. The stove requires priming in order to start.

The exact use of each stove depends upon the manufacturer's recommendations and the type of fuel you use. As a general rule, a windshield is a must, preheating the stove helps it work better, and a stove that has a pump performs better when pumped up. For safety purposes, don't use a

Canister stove

stove in a tent or enclosed area, except when considered absolutely necessary. If you do so, make sure the area is vented, and do everything in your power to avoid fuel leaks. In addition, always change canisters and lines, fill fuel tanks, and prime the stove outside of the shelter.

Plan on ¼ quart of liquid fuel per person per day if you'll need to melt snow for water. Plan on ⅛ quart per person per day if water will be available.

HEADLAMP

A headlamp has become a great alternative and replacement to the old hand-held flashlight. The greatest benefit of a headlamp is that it frees up your hands so that you can use them to meet your other needs. When selecting a headlamp, you should consider its comfort, battery life history, durability, weight, water resistance, and whether it has a tendency to turn on while in a pack. I prefer the newer headlamp style, which has a compact profile, with the battery pack directly behind the bulb.

COOKING POTS

A cooking pot is a luxury item that can be used to cook food and boil water. There are many types available, and the kind you choose should depend on your needs. I recommend a cookware set that includes a frying pan that doubles as a lid, several pots, and a pot gripper or handle. Pots are available in four basic materials:

Aluminum: Aluminum is cheap and the most common material used by backpackers. Unless it has a nonstick coating on the inside of the pan, however, plan on eating scorched food.

Stainless steel: Stainless steel is far more rugged than aluminum but weighs considerably more.

Titanium: Titanium is lighter than aluminum, but the cost may be prohibitive. It has a tendency to blacken your food unless you constantly stir it while cooking.

Composite: Composite cooking pots combine the benefits of aluminum and stainless steel and are durable yet lightweight. The inside of the pan is made from steel to reduce scorching, and aluminum is used on the outside to decrease its weight.

SURVIVAL TIPS

MULTIUSE ITEMS
Whenever able, try to take gear that can serve multiple uses. An example of this would be a durable space blanket (not one of those flimsy cheap ones) that has an orange and a silver side. Not only does it augment your clothing, but it can also be used as a signal, water collection device, and shelter. A military poncho, a heavy-duty garbage bag, and parachute line are a few other examples of multiuse items that you might carry into the wilderness.

TAKE CARE OF YOUR BATTERIES
If batteries become too cold, they may no longer work, making your electronic devices useless. To avoid this, protect your electronic devices by wrapping them in a good insulating material, and use your radiant heat to keep the batteries warm by carrying them between the layers of your clothing.

SLEEPING WARM
Since sleeping bags work by trapping dead air, fluff your bag before you get inside. Exercising and eating a protein snack before bed will help your body produce the needed heat to keep you warm once inside your bag. To avoid inner-bag condensation, keep your mouth and nose uncovered. If conditions are extreme, cover your face with a T-shirt or other porous material.

4

Clothing

Clothing is your first line of defense against the environment. In cold weather, your clothing insulates you, keeping you warm; in hot weather, proper clothing helps keep you cool.

HEAT LOSS

The body is constantly regulating itself in an attempt to keep its thermostat approximately between 97 and 99 degrees F. As heat is lost through radiation, conduction, convection, evaporation, and respiration, you'll need to adjust your clothing to help maintain your body's core temperature.

RADIATION

Heat transfers from your body into the environment through the process of radiation. The head, neck, and hands pose the greatest threat for heat loss due to radiation. Increased clothing will slow the process but doesn't stop it from occurring.

CONDUCTION

Heat is lost from the body through conduction when it comes in contact with any cold item. This poses a significant problem when clothing is soaking wet, and in such circumstances, you should remove and change the clothes or wring out as much moisture as possible.

CONVECTION

Similarly to radiation, convection is a process of heat loss from the body to the surrounding cold air. But unlike radiation, convection would be absent if you were standing completely still and there was absolutely no wind. The wind and your movements cause you to lose heat from convection.

Wearing clothes in a loose and layered fashion will help trap the warm air next to your body, which in turn decreases the heat lost from convection and also insulates you from the environment.

EVAPORATION
Heat is lost through the evaporative process that occurs with perspiration. Monitoring your activity to ensure that you avoid sweating helps. If you are inactive, layered clothing will trap dead air; this will decrease the amount of heat lost through evaporation and actually keep you warmer.

RESPIRATION
Heat is lost through the normal process of breathing. To decrease the heat lost by breathing in cold air, cover or encircle your mouth with a loose cloth. By doing this, you will trap dead air and allow it to warm up slightly prior to breathing it in.

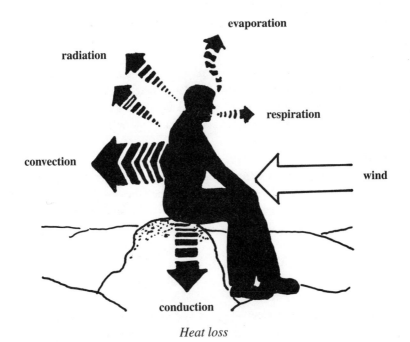

Heat loss

MATERIALS

How well you adjust to heat loss depends on how well your clothes insulate you. Most clothing materials are made of intertwined fibers, which create spaces that trap dead air. Clothes made of down trap air between the feather fibers. As the body loses heat, it is trapped inside the dead air space, and that's how clothes keep you warm. The clothing you select to take on a trip should not only protect you from cold and wet conditions but also provide the breathability needed to avoid overheating. Winter clothes are made from many materials, both natural and synthetic. When choosing clothing for cold climates, it's helpful to understand the characteristics of these materials.

NATURAL FABRICS

Cotton
Cotton has been nicknamed "death cloth," since it loses almost all of its insulating quality when wet. Wet cotton will absorb many times its weight, has extremely poor wicking qualities, and takes forever to dry.

Down
Down is a very good lightweight, natural insulating material. Like cotton, however, down becomes virtually worthless when wet, the feathers clumping together and no longer trapping dead air. The material is best used in dry climates or when you can guarantee it won't get wet.

Wool
Wool retains most of its insulating quality when wet. Wool also retains a lot of the moisture, however, making it extremely heavy when wet. Wool is also fairly effective at protecting you from wind, allowing it to be worn as an outer layer. Its main drawbacks are its weight and bulkiness.

SYNTHETIC FABRICS

Polyester and polypropylene
As a wicking layer polyester and polypropylene wick well, maintain their insulating quality when wet, and dry quickly. As an insulating layer, these

fabrics are lightweight and compressible. They are not very effective at protecting you from the wind, however, and are best accompanied by an outer shell. Common examples of polyester used for the insulating layer are polyester pile and fleece.

Polarguard, Hollofil, and Quallofil

Although these synthetic fibers are most often used in sleeping bags, they can also be found in heavy parkas. Polarguard is composed of sheets, Hollofil of hollow sheets, and Quallofil of hollow sheets that have holes running through the fibers. Basically, Hollofil and Quallofil took Polarguard one step further by creating more insulating dead air space. As with all synthetic fabrics listed, these materials dry quickly and retain most of their insulation quality when wet.

Thinsulate, Microloft, and Primaloft

These thin synthetic fibers create an outstanding lightweight insulation material by allowing more layers. Thinsulate is the heaviest of the three and is most often used in clothing. Microloft and Primaloft are extremely lightweight and are an outstanding alternative to the lightweight down sleeping bag, since they retain their insulation quality when wet.

Nylon

Nylon is a common shell material often used in parkas, rain and wind garments, and mittens. Since nylon is not waterproof, most manufacturers use either special fabrication techniques or treatments to add the feature.

Polyurethane coatings

These inexpensive lightweight coatings protect from outside moisture, but since they are nonbreathable, they don't allow inside moisture to escape. Only use this type of outer garment when physical exertion is at a minimum.

Breathable waterproof coatings

When applied to the inside of a nylon shell, this coating leaves billions of microscopic pores that are large enough for inside vapors to escape yet small enough to keep raindrops out. These coats cost more than those with polyurethane, but less than those with a breathable laminated waterproof membrane.

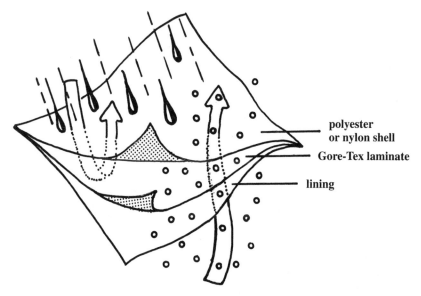

Waterproof breathable nylon

Breathable laminated waterproof membrane

Instead of an inner coating, a separate waterproof and breathable membrane is laminated to the inside of the nylon. The membrane is perforated with millions of microscopic pores that work under the same principle as the waterproof coating. Gore-Tex is the most common example.

In order for the breathable fabrics to be effective, you'll need to keep the pores free of dirt and sweat. In addition, only wash and dry them in accordance with the tag instructions, as some will be ruined if cleaned wrong. Finally, don't expect these breathable coats to be perfect. If your heat output is high and you begin to sweat, this moisture cannot escape any more than the rain can get in. To prevent this, you'll need to wear your clothing in a loose and layered fashion.

COLDER ACRONYM

An acronym that can help you remember how to care for and wear your clothing is COLDER.

CLEAN
Clothes are made of intertwined fibers that, when clean, trap dead air that works as insulation to keep you warm. If clothes are dirty, they lose their ability to insulate you.

AVOID OVERHEATING
Clothes either absorb or repel sweat, causing them to lose their insulating quality or make you wet. In addition, when you become overheated, you lose valuable body heat through evaporation.

LOOSE AND LAYERED
Clothing that is too tight will constrict circulation and predispose you to frostbite. Wearing multiple layers increases the amount of dead air space surrounding the body. It also allows you to add or remove individual layers of clothing as necessary for the given weather conditions. The ability to take

Layers of clothing

a layer off or add it back when needed allows you to avoid getting too cold or overheating by adapting to the climate and the amount of work you are doing. I normally wear three layers: one that wicks moisture away, an insulating layer, and an outer shell.

Wicking layer

Perspiration and moisture wick through this layer, keeping you dry. This is a very important layer, since having wet clothes next to the skin causes twenty-five times greater heat loss than dry ones. Polyester and polypropylene are best for this layer. Cotton is not recommended.

Insulating layer

This layer traps warm air next to the body. Multiple insulating layers may work better than one, as additional air is trapped between them. The best fabrics for this layer are wool, polyester pile, compressed polyester fleece, Hollofil, Quallofil, Polarguard, Thinsulate, Microloft, and Primaloft. Down can be used in dry climates or when you're sure it won't get wet. Sometimes I wear two middle layers, creating another dead air space and providing a finer ability to adjust my layers.

Outer shell

This layer protects you from wind and precipitation. The ideal shell will protect you from getting wet when exposed to rain or snow but has enough ventilation for body moisture to escape. Best for this layer are waterproof coatings that breathe or laminated waterproof membranes that breathe (Gore-Tex). Headgear and gloves are a must, as one-third to one-half of body heat loss occurs from the head and hands.

DRY

Wet clothes lose their insulating quality. To keep the inner layer dry, avoid sweating. Protect your outer layer from moisture by either avoiding exposure to rain or snow or by wearing proper clothing as described above. If your clothes do become wet, dry them by a fire or in the sun. If it's below 32 degrees F and you can't build a fire, let the clothes freeze; once frozen, break the ice out of the clothing. If snow is on your clothes, shake it off; don't brush it off; as this will force the moisture into the fibers.

EXAMINE

Examine your clothing daily for tears and dirt.

REPAIR

Repair any tears as soon as they occur. This may require a needle and thread, so make sure you pack them.

PARKA AND RAIN PANTS

A parka and rain pants are needed for protection from moisture and wind. They will normally be made from nylon with a polyurethane coating, a waterproof coating that breathes, or a laminated waterproof membrane that breathes (Gore-Tex). In some cases, a parka will come with an insulating garment that can be zipped inside. Besides the material, there are other criteria to consider when choosing these garments:

APPROPRIATE SIZE

These garments should be big enough that you can comfortably add wicking and insulating layers underneath without compromising your movement. In addition, the parka's lower end should extend beyond your hips to keep moisture away from the top of your pants.

DUAL SEPARATING ZIPPERS

Look for zippers that separate at both ends.

VENTILATION ADJUSTMENT

Parkas should have openings for ventilation in front, at your waist, under your arms, and at your wrist. For rain pants, the openings should be located in the front and along the outside of the lower legs, extending to about mid-calf, making it easier to put on or remove your boots. For females, there are pants available with a zipper that extends down and around the crotch. The added benefit is obvious. These openings can be adjusted with zippers, Velcro, or drawstrings.

SEALED SEAMS

Seams should be taped or well bonded, or they will allow moisture to penetrate through the clothing.

ACCESSIBLE POCKETS
What good is a pocket if you can't get to it? In addition, make sure the openings have protective rain baffles.

BRIMMED HOOD AND NECK FLAP
A brimmed hood will help channel moisture away from the eyes and face. In addition, a neck flap will help prevent radiant body heat loss from the neck area.

BOOTS
Boots are a very important part of your clothing. Always choose the right type for your needs, and break the boots in before your trip. When selecting boots, consider the type of travel you intend to do. I have four styles that I use, and each serves a different purpose. They are leather, lightweight leather/fabric, plastic, and rubber.

LEATHER BOOTS
Leather boots are ideal all-purpose boots. A stiff upper provides protection for the ankle, and a hard sole will help when kick-stepping and technical climbing. For extreme conditions, you'll need to treat them with a waterproofing material (read the manufacturer's directions on how this should be done) and wear a comfortable, protective wool-blend sock. Another popular option in leather boots is an added Thinsulate and Gore-Tex liner, which helps protect your feet from the cold and moist conditions. If you elect to use Thinsulate or Gore-Tex, be sure you follow the manufacturer's directions explicitly on how to care for and treat the boots. If oils soak through the leather and into the lining, they will nullify their insulating qualities.

LIGHTWEIGHT LEATHER/FABRIC BOOTS
The lightweight leather/fabric boot is a popular fair-weather boot, since it is lighter and dries faster than the leather boot. On the downside, moisture easily soaks through the fabric, these boots provide less stability for your ankle, and on difficult terrain, they are not rigid enough for a good kick-step and not generally hard enough to be worn with crampons or snowshoes.

PLASTIC BOOTS

Plastic waterproof boots are ideal when traveling on hard snow and when conditions require kick-stepping or crampon use for long periods of time. This extremely stiff boot has a removable inner insulating boot that can be quickly dried. Although your feet will get hot and sometimes the liner will get wet from perspiration, the heat will be trapped by the plastic, keeping your feet warm.

RUBBER BOOTS

Rubber boots are most often used for nontechnical extreme cold-weather conditions. They normally have nylon uppers with molded rubber bottoms and removable felt inner boots. As with the plastic boots, the inner boots can be easily removed and dry quickly.

Keeping your boots clean will help them protect you better. For leather and lightweight leather/fabric boots, wash off dirt and debris using a mild soap that doesn't damage leather. For plastic and rubber boots, wash and dry the liners, and clean all dirt and debris from the outer boots.

SOCKS

Socks need to provide adequate insulation, reduce friction, and wick away and absorb moisture from the skin. Socks most often are made of wool, polyester, nylon, or an acrylic material. Wool tends to dry more slowly than the other materials but is still a great option. Cotton should be avoided, as it loses its insulating qualities when wet. For best results, wear two pairs of socks. The inner sock (often made of polyester) wicks the moisture away from the foot; the outer sock (often a wool blend) provides the insulation that keeps your feet warm. Gore-Tex socks are often worn over the outer pair during extremely wet conditions. Keep your feet dry, and change your socks at least once a day. If any hot spots develop on your feet, immediately apply moleskin before they become blisters.

GAITERS

When traveling in snow or wet conditions, you don't want moisture to enter your boots over the top cuffs. Full-length gaiters will help prevent this from occurring by covering your lower legs from the boots' lower laces to just above the calf muscles. Most gaiters are made of Gore-Tex or a similar breathable material that is waterproof yet allows perspiration to escape. Gaiters are often held together with Velcro, snaps, or zippers. If the gaiters have zippers, make sure they are strong and have protective covering flaps.

HAND COVERINGS

Since a fair amount of heat is lost from the hands, it is best to keep them covered with gloves or mittens. Gloves encase each individual finger and allow you the dexterity to perform many of your daily tasks. Mittens encase the second through fifth fingers, decreasing your dexterity, but increasing hand warmth from the captured radiant heat. Which you should wear depends on your activity. To get the best of both worlds, I insert my gloved hands inside mittens. I remove just the mittens when I need to work with my hands. My gloves are made from a polyester fleece or a wool-synthetic blend. My mittens are made from a waterproof yet breathable fabric, like Gore-Tex.

HEADGEAR

Since over 50 percent of your body heat is lost through the head, you'll need to keep it covered. There are many types of headgear, and your activity and the elements will dictate which one you choose. As a general rule, there are two basic categories: rain hats and insulating hats.

RAIN HAT

A rain hat is often made from nylon or an insulation material with an outer nylon covering. For added waterproof and breathable characteristics, Gore-Tex is often used. For extra protection, choose a hat that has earflaps, which can be used in extreme conditions.

INSULATING HAT

An insulating hat is made from wool, polypropylene, or polyester fleece. The most common styles of these are the watch cap and the balaclava. The balaclava is a great option, since it can cover the head, ears, and neck (front and back side), yet leaves an opening for your face.

Because so much heat is lost through the head, headgear *should not* be the first thing you take off when you are overheating. Mild adjustments—

such as opening the zipper to your coat—will allow for the gradual changes needed to avoid sweating. In cold conditions, headgear should be removed only when other options have not cooled you down enough.

EYE PROTECTION

Goggles or sunglasses with side shields that filter out UV wavelengths are a must for travel in snow environments. It doesn't take long to burn the eyes, and once this occurs, you will have several days of eye pain, along with light sensitivity, tearing, and a foreign body sensation. Since the symptoms of the burn usually don't show up for four to six hours after the exposure, you can get burned and not even realize it is happening. Once a burn occurs, you'll need to get out of the light, remove contacts if wearing them, and cover the eyes with a sterile dressing until the light sensitivity subsides. If pain medication is available, you'll probably need to use it. Once healed, make sure to protect the eyes to prevent another burn. If no goggles or sunglasses are available, improvise by using either a man-made or natural material that covers the eyes, with a narrow horizontal slit for each eye.

ZIPPERS

Zippers on garments and sleeping bags often break or get stuck. Under mild conditions, this may not present a great problem. In a cold-weather environment, however, you can lose a lot of body heat when you are unable to close a zipper properly. To decrease the odds of zipper problems, your gear should have zippers with a dual separating system (separates at both ends) and teeth made from a material that won't rust or freeze, such as polyester. Your zippers should also be waterproof. If they don't have a baffle covering, apply a waterproof coating to the zipper's backing. The latter option has the advantages of lighter weight and easier access to the zipper.

SKIN PROTECTION

Ultraviolet (UV) radiation that reflects off snow and ice is very intense, and it can cause painful and potentially debilitating and sunburn during travel in a snow or ice environment. The best way to avoid this problem is to wear protective clothing. For skin that cannot be covered, use a sunscreen or sunblock. These products are available in various sun protection factor (SPF) ratings, which indicate how much longer than normal you can be exposed to

UV radiation prior to burning. They work by absorbing the UV radiation. Sunblock reflects the UV radiation and is most often used in sensitive areas where intense exposure might occur, like the ears and nose. You'll need to constantly reapply these products throughout the day, as their effectiveness is lost over time and due to sweating.

SURVIVAL TIPS

AVOIDING FROZEN BOOTS

To avoid the dreaded morning ritual of putting on stiff, frozen boots, before bed place your boots inside a stuff sack that is turned inside out, and sleep with them behind the bend in your knees.

SLEEPING WARM

Remove all damp or wet clothes before going to bed. Place those that are slightly damp inside your bag behind the bend in your knees to be dried by your radiant heat.

5

Camping

A shelter is your second line of personal protection. Its primary purpose is to protect you from the elements: cold, heat, wet, and wind. The type of shelter used and its relative importance are determined by the climate.

SELECTING A CAMPSITE

When selecting a campsite, make sure it provides the resources necessary to meet your needs. To find the ideal site, consider the following criteria:

LOCATION AND SIZE

Your site should be on a level surface and be big enough for both you and your equipment.

OPTIMIZE THE SUN'S WARMTH

Position the shelter so that it has a southern exposure if it's north of the equator, or a northern exposure if south of it; this allows for optimal light and heat from the sun throughout the day. In addition, try to position the door so that it faces east, since an east-side opening will allow for best early-morning sun exposure.

AVOID WIND PROBLEMS

Since wind can wrap over the top of a tent and through its opening, do not place the door in the wind's path or on the opposite side of the wind's travel. Instead, have the door positioned at 90 degrees to the prevailing wind. Avoid ridgetops and open areas. When setting up your tent, secure it in place by staking it down. It doesn't take much of a wind to move or destroy your shelter.

USE THE SNOW'S INSULATION

If in snow, dig down to bare ground whenever possible. The ground's radiant heat will help keep you warmer at night. Keep the inside of your tent dry by brushing snow off your clothing and removing your snowshoes, skis, and boots (you may need to do this in the vestibule) prior to entering.

WATER SOURCE

In order to avoid having to melt snow for water, if a stream or lake is close by, build your shelter 100 feet or so from it.

SAFETY FIRST

Avoid sites with the potential for environmental hazards that can wipe out all your hard work in just a matter of seconds. These include avalanche slopes; drainages and dry riverbeds with a potential for flash floods; rock formations that might collapse; dead trees that might blow down; overhanging dead limbs; and large animal trails. If near bodies of water, stay above tide marks.

SURVIVAL

In an emergency, make sure your camp is located next to a signal and recovery site. (Refer to chapter 7 for signaling details.)

TENT

The majority of tents are made of nylon and held up with aluminum poles. Tents need to be waterproof and breathable—waterproof to prevent moisture from entering from the outside, and breathable to avoid condensation formation on the inside. Nylon is not waterproof, so some manufacturers use a breathable waterproof coating or a breathable laminated waterproof membrane for the tent's inner wall. Both of these options allow moisture to escape but prevent outside moisture from entering. If an outer wall is used, this is not necessary. To make the outer wall water repellent, a polyurethane coating is often added. Some tents come with UV protection and even have a fire-retardant finish. The tent's seams will either have a tape weld or require that you apply a seam sealant before its first use. Follow the manufacturer's recommendations on how to seal the tent's seams. A tent's poles need to be durable enough to handle the wind and snow with-

Commercial tent

out bending or breaking. For general use, get poles that have a diameter of 8.5 millimeters. For extreme conditions, use a 9-millimeter or greater pole to add more durability to the tent's frame.

A tent's size, strength, and weight will all factor into your decision on which one to use. A tradeoff between weight and strength is often foremost in people's minds. When choosing a tent, you'll have to decide which is more important: less weight on your back or more durability and comfort in camp. I'd advise against a single-walled tent, unless it has multiple vents that can be opened to prevent inner condensation moisture. A double-walled tent provides a breathable inner wall and an outer waterproof rain fly. Since moisture from inside the tent will escape through the breathable wall and collect on the inside of the rain fly, the two walls should not touch, or the moisture will not escape and condensation will form inside the tent. The ideal rain fly will allow for a small area of protection—between the door and outside—commonly called a vestibule. This area allows for extra storage, boot removal, and cooking. For information on zippers, see chapter 4.

Most tents are classified as three-season or four-season tents. There are also combo tents that can be used as either.

THREE-SEASON TENTS
Three-season tents are normally lighter and often have see-through mesh panels, which provide ventilation.

FOUR-SEASON TENTS
Four-season tents are made from solid panels and in general are heavier and stronger. Typically, they have stronger poles and reinforced seams.

COMBO TENTS
Some tents are marketed to be used in either three or four seasons by providing a solid panel that can be zipped shut over the ventilating mesh.

BIVOUAC BAG

The original concept of bivouac bags was to allow the backpacker or mountaineer an emergency lightweight shelter. However, even though these shelters are made for just one person, many travelers now carry them as their

Bill Frye sets up a bivouac.

primary three-season shelter. A good bag will be made from a breathable waterproof fabric such as Gore-Tex or Tetra-Tex, with a coated nylon floor. A hoop or flexible wire sewn across the head area, along with nonremovable mosquito netting, is advised for comfort and venting when needed. For information on zippers, see chapter 4.

EMERGENCY TARP SHELTERS

An emergency shelter can be made using your rain fly or a tarp, should other options not be available. The exact type of shelter you should build depends on the environment, available materials, and time. Your shelter site should be large enough for both you and your equipment, close to resources, and located away from potential safety hazards. Regardless of the type you build, tarp shelters need to have a 45- to 60-degree angle on all sides. If you have two tarps, a rain fly can be erected over the first to increase your protection from the elements.

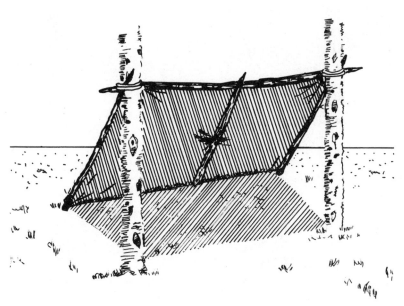

Tarp lean-to

Tarp A-frame

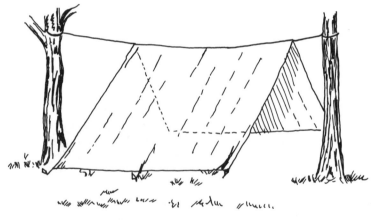

Tarp A-tent

EMERGENCY NATURAL SHELTERS

EMERGENCY TREE PIT

A tree pit shelter is a quick, immediate-action shelter used in forested snow environments. The optimal tree has multiple lower branches—like a Douglas or grand fir—that protect its base from the snow and rain. Pine trees provide little protection and are not a good choice. As the snow level

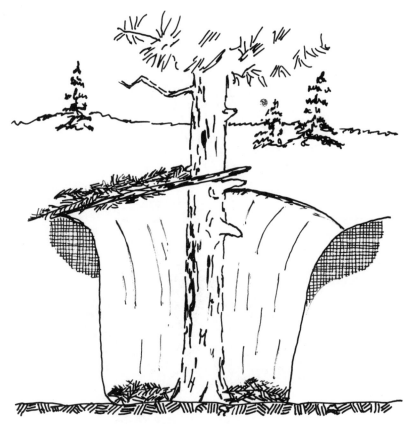

Tree pit

rises around the tree, it creates an excellent source of insulation for your shelter. To make a tree pit, remove the snow from the tree's base, making an area big enough for you and your equipment. If able, dig until you reach bare ground, and remove obstructive branches, which can be used for added overhead cover—protecting you from the elements.

THERMAL A-FRAME
A thermal A-frame is most often used in the warm temperate and snow environments, where there is an abundance of trees and snow. Find a tree with a forked branch that's 3 to 4 feet above the base of its trunk after you

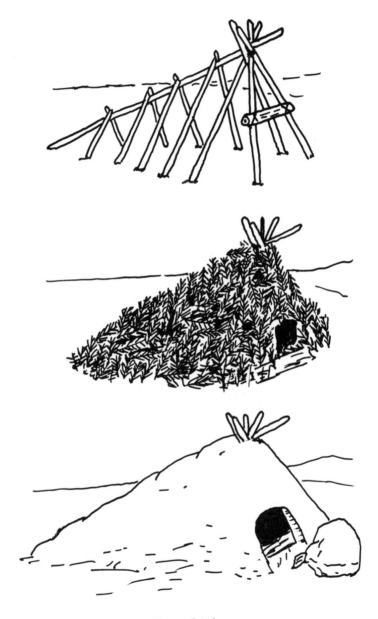

Thermal A-frame

Dawn-Marie Davenport emerging from a thermal A-frame

have dug down to bare ground. Break away any other branches that pose a threat or interfere with the construction of your A-frame. Place a ridgepole (a fallen tree 12 to 15 feet long and the diameter of your wrist) into the forked branch, forming a 30-degree angle between the pole and the ground. If you're unable to find a tree with a forked branch, lash the ridgepole to the tree. Other options are to locate a fallen tree that's at an appropriate 30-degree angle to the ground, or to lay a strong ridgepole against a 3- to 4-foot-high stump. Lay support poles across the ridgepole, on both sides, at a 60-degree angle to the ground. Support poles need to be long enough to extend above the ridgepole *slightly,* and they should be placed approximately 1 to 1½ feet apart. If the support poles end up above the roof material, moisture will run down them and into your shelter. Crisscross small branches into the support poles. Cover the framework with any available grass, moss, boughs, and so forth. Place the materials in a layered fashion, starting at the bottom. Finally, throw at least 8 inches (you may add more, but this is the minimum) of snow over the top of the shelter. Cover the door opening with your pack or similar item.

OPPOSING LEAN-TO

A large, opposing lean-to can easily be built by using natural materials commonly found in warm temperate and snow environments. A double lean-to provides protection from all directions. Find two trees approximately 7 to 8 feet apart, with forked branches 5 to 6 feet high on each trunk. Break away any of the branches that pose a safety threat or interfere with the construction process, and also clear any saplings, duff, or wood that is between the two trees and may interfere with construction. Place a ridgepole (a strong, wrist-diameter pole that's long enough to span between the two trees) into the forked branches. If you're unable to find two trees with forked branches, use a square lash to attach the ridgepole to the trees.

Lay several support poles across the ridgepole, on each side and at a 45- to 60-degree angle to the ground. Support poles need to be long enough to provide this angle and yet barely extend beyond the top of the ridgepole.

Opposing lean-to

Incorporate both the front and back into the framework, leaving enough room for a small doorway on either side. The doorway can be covered with your pack or a snow block when needed. To create a stronger framework, weave small branches into and perpendicular to the support poles. Cover the entire shelter with 12 to 18 inches of boughs, bark, duff, and snow, in that order, depending on availability of resources. Place the material in a layered fashion, starting at the bottom. Make a vent hole in the top if you plan to have a small fire inside. If you've used snow in the lean-to's construction, don't get the temperature inside your shelter above 32 degrees F, or it will start to melt.

SNOW CAVE

A snow cave is most often used in warm temperate (winter) and snow environments and is a quick and easily constructed one- or two-man shelter. When using these shelters, the outside temperature must be well below freezing to ensure that the walls of the cave will stay firm and the snow will not melt. Never get the inside temperature above freezing, or the shelter will lose its insulating quality, and you'll get wet from the subsequent moisture. With this in mind, these shelters are not designed for large groups, since the radiant heat will raise the temperature above freezing, making it a dangerous environment. As a general rule of thumb, if you cannot see your breath, the shelter is too warm. When constructing the cave, use the COLDER principle and take care not to overheat or get wet.

To construct a snow cave, find an area with firm snow at a depth of at least 6 feet (a steep slope such as a snowdrift will suffice, provided there is no risk of an avalanche). Dig an entryway into the slope deep enough to start a tunnel (approximately 3 feet) and wide enough for you to fit into. Since cold air sinks, construct a snow platform 2 to 3 feet above the entryway. It should be flat, level, and large enough for you to comfortably lie down on. Using the entryway as a starting point, hollow out a domed area that is large enough for you and your equipment. To prevent the ceiling from settling or falling in, create a high domed roof. To prevent asphyxiation, make a ventilation hole in the roof. For best results, the hole should be at a 45-degree angle to your sleeping platform (creating an imaginary triangle between the platform, the door, and the hole). If available, insert a stick or pole through the hole so that it can be cleared periodically. To

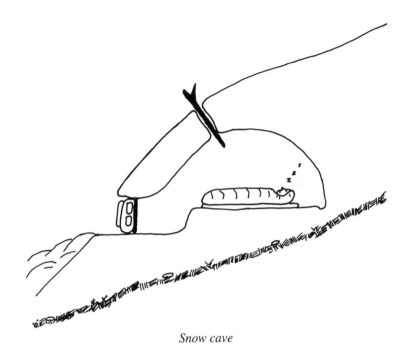

Snow cave

further protect the shelter from the elements, place a block of snow or your pack in the entryway. Since you are oblivious to the conditions outside, check the entrance periodically.

SNOW A-FRAME

A snow A-frame shelter is most often used in the warm temperate winter, snow, and ice environments where the snow has been windblown and firmly packed. To make a snow A-frame, find an 8-by-4-foot flat area that is clear of trees and underbrush. The snow must be at least 3 to 4 feet deep. Stomp out a rectangular platform that's wide and long enough to accommodate your body, and let it harden for at least thirty minutes. Dig a 3-foot-deep entryway just in front of the rectangular area. Evacuate the compacted snow by cutting multiple 3-foot-square blocks that are 8 to 10 inches wide; this will require an instrument like a snow saw, large machete, stick, or ski. Once the blocks have been removed, place them one against the other to

Snow A-frame

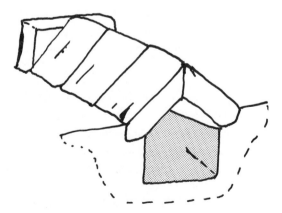

Snow A-frame

form an A-frame above the trench. For best results, cut one of the first opposing blocks in half lengthwise. This will make it easier to place the additional blocks on—one at a time versus trying to continually lay two against one another. Fill in any gaps with surrounding snow, and cover the doorway.

A quick and easy variation of the snow A-frame shelter can be made when the snow is not wind-packed and a snow cave is not an option. Simply dig a trench as described above, but make one side higher than the other; cover it with a lean-to type framework of branches or similar material; and then add a thick layer of snow as roofing.

IGLOO
An igloo can provide a long-term winter shelter for a small family. This shelter is normally used in areas where the snow is windblown and firmly packed. An igloo that has a diameter of 8 feet is adequate for one person; a diameter of 12 feet can easily house four people. Its construction requires a snow saw or large knife.

Find a windblown snowdrift or field, 2 feet deep, firm enough that it will support your weight with only a slight indent. Draw a circle in the snow that represents the desired igloo size. The marked outline will become the inside diameter of the igloo. Establish a door location, which should be at a 90-degree angle to the wind. Make two parallel lines in the snow that are 30 inches apart and perpendicular to the door entrance. These lines should extend one-third of the way toward the center of the circle and an equal distance away. This area will eventually become your entrance, cooking, and storage area. Since cold air sinks, it also serves as a cold sump for the shelter. Using the two lines as your guide, cut blocks that measure 30 inches long, 15 inches deep, and 8 to 12 inches thick. Start at the outside of the circle and continue until the two parallel lines end (one-third of the way to the center of the circle). Set the blocks aside. In order to finish the shelter, you will need to acquire additional blocks from another location. Once all the blocks are cut, you can begin building the igloo.

Start by placing four full-size blocks, side by side, on the outside of the circle. Next, make a diagonal cut that runs from the ground of the second block to the top of the fourth. The fifth and following blocks will be the standard 15-inch height. The slope will provide a spiral effect that makes the construction easier and provides stability to the igloo. Continue adding

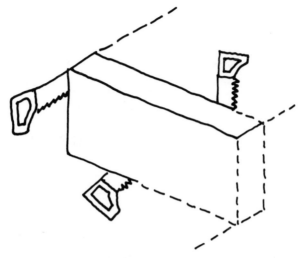

Cutting a snow block

blocks until the first layer is complete. You may need to add support pillars
under the blocks that go over the entrance. As your dome begins to take
form, trim the blocks (see illustration) and tilt them slightly inward to
increase the contact and stability. In addition, greater stability is obtained
if each block placed doesn't end on the same seam as the one below it (you
may need to trim one or two blocks to avoid this).

As the dome wall gets higher, you'll need to work from inside the igloo,
exiting through the doorway created when the blocks were cut. The last
layers of blocks need to be trimmed at an angle so the key block can be

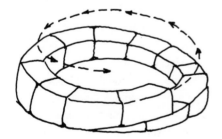
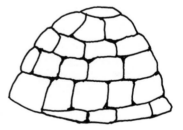

Constructing an igloo

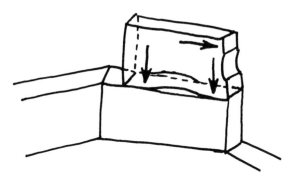

Trimming the blocks for a better fit

positioned on top. The key, or final, block is the centerpiece. It is round and tapered in from the top toward the shelter.

To finish the igloo, use snow as the mortar to close all weak areas. If you want to increase the insulation quality of the shelter, simply pile more snow around it. Create a roof over the entryway similar to that described for the snow A-frame variation, above. If you intend to have a small fire, don't forget a vent hole, and don't allow the temperature inside the igloo to get too warm. You should be able to see your breath.

MOLDED DOME

A variation of the snow cave and igloo is a molded dome, used in conditions where the snow is not wind-packed and a snow cave is not an option. Use your gear, boughs, or other material to create a cone that will serve as the foundation to your shelter. Pile snow on top of the cone until you have a dome that is approximately 5 feet high and has at least 3 feet of snow covering the inner core. Smooth the outer surface, and let the snow sit for one to two hours so that it can settle (the time frame depends on your weather conditions). Since 18 inches is an ideal insulating depth for a molded dome, gather multiple 2-foot-long branches and insert them into the dome, pointing toward its center, leaving approximately 6 inches exposed. Decide where you'd like your entryway, and dig a 3-foot-deep entry tunnel. Dig approximately one-third of the way toward the center of the molded dome, or until you reach the core material. Remove the gear, boughs, or other material, and hollow out the inside, using the 2-foot branches you inserted as your guide for inner-wall thickness.

Molded dome

Molded dome

SURVIVAL TIPS

HEAT INSIDE SNOW SHELTERS

If the temperature in a shelter made partially or completely of snow exceeds 32 degrees F, it will begin to melt and will get you and your equipment wet. As a general rule of thumb, as long as you can see your breath, the temperature is probably not too high.

AVOIDING CARBON DIOXIDE (CO_2) POISONING

If you intend to use any heating device inside an enclosed shelter, make sure to create a vent hole that will allow the CO_2 to escape. This is usually placed at a 45-degree angle between the top of the shelter and the shelter's opening.

INCREASING THE INSULATION VALUE
OF A COLD-WEATHER SHELTER

Once your shelter is complete, you may elect to add a snow wall on the windward side to decrease the wind's effects on your site.

STAKING OUT A TENT OR PONCHO SHELTER

In deep snow, you may have to use dead-men to secure your shelter sides in place. Tie one end of a piece of line to the shelter material, and secure its other end to a 1-inch-diameter branch that is about 6 inches long. Pull the attached line at a 90-degree angle to the wrinkles in the shelter's material and secure the branch in place. To do this, kick a small hole in the snow, jam the line and branch into it, and, while holding the branch in place, cover it with snow. These dead-men work great when temperatures are below freezing, but when the sun is out, if the temperature gets above freezing, these anchors may pop free, and your shelter will fall down.

CREATING A COOKING PIT OR COMMUNITY AREA

Digging a 6-foot-deep round hole, along with a sitting platform 2 feet up from the bottom, creates a wonderful, wind-blocked area for cooking and community gatherings.

6

Fire and Other Heat Sources

Fire is the third line of personal protection and, in most cases, will not be necessary if you've adequately met your clothing and shelter needs. In extreme conditions, however, fire is very beneficial for warding off hypothermia and other exposure injuries. Fire serves many other functions as well: providing light, warmth, and comfort; a source of heat for cooking, purifying water, and drying clothes; and a means of signaling. In addition, a fire is relaxing and helps reduce stress. For some of these purposes, building a fire is not always necessary. You might instead use a backpacking stove, Sterno stove, or solid compressed fuel tablets.

MAN-MADE HEAT SOURCES

A man-made heat source can be used in any of your various shelters, provided there is proper ventilation. However, if you are in a tent, limit its use to the vestibule area to avoid fuel spills or burning the tent. In addition, if you're inside a natural or thermal shelter, do not allow the temperature to get above 32 degrees F; you should always be able to see your breath.

BACKPACKING STOVE

The two basic styles of backpacking stoves are canister and liquid fuel. Canister designs use butane, propane, or isobutane cartridges as their fuel source. The most common types of liquid fuels used are white gas and kerosene. (For more details on the various styles of backpacking stoves, see chapter 3.)

STERNO

Sterno has been around for a long time and still has a place for many backcountry explorers. The fuel is a jellied alcohol that comes in a 7-ounce can.

Under normal conditions, it has a two-hour burn time. Although far inferior to a good backpacking stove for cooking, it is very effective at warming water and a shelter in an emergency. An inexpensive folding stove is made for use with Sterno, but with a little imagination, you can create your own.

SOLID COMPRESSED FUEL TABLETS

Esbit, Trioxane, and Hexamine are the three basic tablets on the market. Esbit is the newest of the three, and unlike its predecessors, it is nontoxic. This nonexplosive, virtually odorless and smokeless tablet can generate up to 1,400 degrees F of intense heat, providing twelve to fifteen minutes of usable burn time per cube. When used with a commercial or improvised stove, it can *sometimes* boil a pint of water in less than eight minutes. These tablets easily light from a spark and can also be used as tinder to start a fire.

BUILDING A FIRE

When man-made heat sources are either not available or don't meet your needs, you may elect to build a fire. Always use a safe site, and put the fire completely out, so that it is cold to the touch, before you leave. Locate the fire in close proximity to fire materials and your shelter. It should be built on flat, level ground and have adequate protection from the elements. Before starting the fire, prepare the site by clearing a 3-foot fire circle, scraping away all leaves, brush, debris, and snow, down to bare ground if possible. To successfully build a fire, you need to have all three elements of the fire triangle present—heat, oxygen, and fuel—although your fuels will vary depending on what is on hand.

HEAT

Heat is required to start the fire. Since matches and lighters often fail and will eventually run out, you must consider alternative sources of heat to start your fire. One good option is to use a sparker, or metal match, which virtually never runs out.

Matches

Matches run out, get wet, and never seem to work in a time of crisis. If you are dead set on using matches anyway, I recommend NATO-issue survival matches, which have hand-dipped and varnished heads that are supposed to light even when wet and exposed to strong wind or rain. These matches will burn around twelve seconds—enough time to light most fires. In order to protect the match from going out, light it between cupped hands while positioning your body to block the flame from the wind and rain. Regardless of the type you carry, store your matches in a waterproof container until ready for use.

Lighters

Lighters are a form of flint and steel, with an added fuel source that keeps the flame going. Like matches, they have a tendency to fail when used during inclement weather, and once the fuel is used up, they become dead weight. If you understand a lighter's shortcomings and still elect to use one, I recommend a Colibri Quantum, the Cadillac of lighters. These high-end lighters are water-resistant and shockproof, ignite at high altitudes, and are marketed as wind-resistant. To use, simply place the flame directly onto the tinder.

Metal match (artificial flint)

A metal match is similar to the flint used in a cigarette lighter, but much bigger. When stroked with an object, the friction creates a long spark that can be used to light tinder. Most metal matches are made from a mixture of metals and rare earth elements. The mixture is alloyed at a high temperature and then shaped into rods of various diameters.

To use a metal match, place it in the center of your tinder, and while holding it firmly in place with one hand, use the opposite hand to strike it with your knife blade, using a firm yet controlled downward stroke at 90 degrees. The resulting spark should provide enough heat to ignite the tinder. This may take several attempts. If, after five tries, it has not lit, rework the tinder to ensure that adequate edges are exposed and oxygen is able to flow through it. The S.O.S. Strike Force is the most popular commercial metal match available. There also are two one-hand-use metal matches on the market: the Spark-Lite and the BlastMatch.

S.O.S. Strike Force

This metal match has a ½-inch round alloy flint attached to a hollow, hard plastic handle that houses emergency tinder. It also has a flint cover with a hardened steel striker attached, making this system completely self-sufficient. Although the system is a little bulky, it weighs slightly less than 4 ounces.

The Spark-Lite

The Spark-Lite is small and lightweight, measuring approximately 2¼ by 9/32 by 9/32 inches. Its spark is also smaller than that of the larger metal matches. It has a serrated wheel, similar to that on a cigarette lighter, that strikes a small flint when stroked. In order to make this a one-hand-use item, the flint is spring-loaded, maintaining contact with the wheel at all times. The small flint is supposed to allow for approximately a thousand strokes before it runs out. To use, stroke the sparking wheel with your thumb while holding the Spark-Lite's body with your fingers of the same hand.

BlastMatch

The BlastMatch is larger and weighs more than the Spark-Lite, measuring 4 by 1⅜ by ⅞ inches. It has a much larger, molded plastic body that holds a 2½-inch-long by ½-inch-diameter rod of flint. The flint is spring-loaded, and when the cap is released, the flint is propelled out. To use, place the flint tip in the center of your tinder, apply pressure to the side catch with your thumb, and push the body downward. This action will force the scraper, located inside the catch, down the flint, creating a large spark.

Pyrotechnics

Flares should be used only as a last resort in starting fires. It's best to save these signaling devices for their intended use. However, if you are unable to start a fire, and the risk of hypothermia is present, a flare is a very effective heat source. Its use is simple: After preparing the tinder, safely ignite it by lighting the flare and directing its flames onto the tinder. Time is of the essence, so prepare your firelay in advance, leaving an opening large enough that you can direct the flare's flame onto the underlying tinder.

OXYGEN

Oxygen is necessary for the fuel to burn, and it needs to be present at all stages of a fire. To ensure this, you'll need a platform and brace. A platform is any dry material that protects your fuel from the ground or snow.

Snow platform and brace

During extremely wet conditions or when there is a heavy snow covering, a platform can be made by laying multiple green logs next to one another. Building the fire on the green logs will protect it from the snow or moist ground. A brace is usually a wrist-diameter branch that allows oxygen to circulate through the fuel when the fuel is leaned against it. This will prevent the snow from putting the fire out.

FUEL
Fuel can be separated into three categories—tinder, kindling, and fuel— each building upon the previous one.

Tinder
Tinder is any material that will light from a spark. It's extremely valuable in getting the larger stages of fuel lit. There are two types of tinders: man-made and natural.

Man-made tinder
When venturing into the wilderness, always carry man-made tinder in your survival kit. If you should become stranded during harsh weather conditions,

it may prove to be the key in having or not having a fire that first night. Since it is a one-time-use item, immediately start gathering natural tinder so that it can be dried out and prepared for use once your man-made tinder is used up. For natural tinder to work, it needs to be dry, have edges, and allow oxygen to circulate within it. However, for man-made tinder, this is not always the case, and the key might be as simple as scraping or fluffing it so it can catch a spark. The most common man-made forms of tinder are petroleum-based, compressed tinder tabs, and solid compressed fuel tablets (discussed under Man-Made Heat Sources, above).

Petroleum-Based Tinder

There are many examples of this product, but perhaps the most common is the Tinder-Quik tab. It is waterproof, odorless, and made from a light, compressible fiber that is impregnated with beeswax, petroleum, and silicones. To use it, simply fluff the fiber up so that it has edges to catch a spark. The

Cotton balls and Vaseline easily catch a spark and light.

tinder will burn for approximately two minutes. Although Tinder-Quik was designed for use with the Spark-Lite flint system, described above, it can be used with any heat source. Less expensive, homemade petroleum-based tinder can be made with 100 percent cotton balls that are saturated with petroleum jelly and stuffed into a 35-millimeter film canister. This tinder is very effective, even under harsh wet and windy conditions.

Compressed Tinder Tabs
WetFire tinder tablets are perhaps the most common compressed tinder tablets. Each tablet is waterproof, nontoxic, odorless, smokeless, and burns around 1,300 degrees F for two to three minutes. Unlike the Tinder-Quik tabs, it is not compressible. To use, I prepare the tinder by making a few small shavings to catch my metal match sparks.

Natural Tinder
For natural tinder to work, it generally needs to be dry, have edges, and allow oxygen to circulate within it. Gather natural tinder before you need it so that you have time to dry it in the sun, between your clothing, or by a fire—and keep it dry until you need it. There are three basic types of natural tinder: bark; scrapings; and grass, ferns, and lichen. If you are uncertain whether something will work for tinder, try it. Always remove any wet bark or pith before breaking the tinder down, and keep it off the wet ground during and after preparation. Since some tinder will collect moisture from the air, always prepare it last.

Bark
Prepare layered forms of tinder by working them between your hands and fingers until they're light and airy; To do this, start by holding a long section of the bark with both hands. Use a back and forth twisting action, working the bark until it becomes fibrous. Next, place the fibrous bark between the palms of your hands and roll your hands back and forth until the bark becomes thin, light, and airy. At this point you should be able to light them from a spark. In most cases, I prepare this tinder until I have enough to form a small bird's nest. Many types of bark will work as tinder, but my favorite is birch. Birch bark will light even when wet due to a highly flammable resin in it.

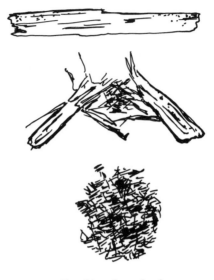

Breaking down bark

Wood scrapings

Wood scrapings are created by repeatedly running your knife blade, at a 90-degree angle, across a flat section of dead pitch wood or heartwood. To be effective, you'll need enough scrapings to fill the palm of your hand. Like birch bark, pitch wood will also light even when wet. The high concentration of pitch in the wood's fibers makes it highly flammable.

Grass, ferns, and lichen

As with bark, I create a bird's nest with these materials, sometimes breaking them down further and sometimes not, depending on the situation. This form of tinder needs to be completely dry to achieve success.

Kindling

Kindling is usually composed of twigs or wood shavings that range in diameter from pencil lead to pencil thickness. It should easily light when placed on a small flame. Sources include small, dead twigs found on the dead branches at the bottom of many trees and shavings from larger pieces of dry dead wood. You may also use heavy cardboard or gasoline- or oil-soaked wood.

Making wood scrapings

Wood scrapings provide good tinder.

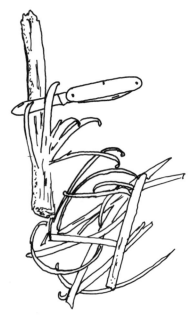

Wood shavings

Fuel

Fuel is any material that is thumb-size or bigger that will burn slowly and steadily once lit. Kinds of fuel include dry, standing dead wood and branches; dead heartwood (the dry inside portion of a fallen tree trunk or large branches); green wood that is finely split; dry grasses twisted into bunches; and dry animal dung. Dead heartwood works best when obtained from a tree that died a natural death (unlike one that has been cut with a chainsaw). These stumps tend to have pointed tops that do not allow snow and moisture to collect and eventually saturate the inner wood. In addition, certain coniferous trees that die from natural causes will contain large amounts of pitch. This wood is commonly called pitch wood and is a great find when you are cold and in need of a quick fire, since it lights easily, even under the worst conditions.

Access this wood by any means available, such as cutting with an ax or big knife; using a pry pole to separate large splinters of the wood; or kicking the stump. Break down the larger pieces with your knife or ax.

STEPS TO BUILDING A FIRE

When building a fire, it is important to gather enough fuel to build three knee-high fires. This allows you to go back to a previous stage if the fire starts to die and to keep the fire going while you get more material. Once the wood or other fuel is gathered, break it down from big to small, always preparing the smallest stages last. This will help decrease the amount of moisture your tinder and kindling collect during the preparation process. If conditions are wet, you'll need to strip off all lichen and bark, and for best results, split the branches in half to expose the dry inner wood. Build a platform and brace, as described above under Oxygen, and use the brace to keep your various stages of fuel off the ground while breaking it down.

Once all the stages of fuel are prepared, either light or place the lit tinder on the platform next to the brace. Use the brace to place your smaller kindling directly over the flame. Spread a handful of kindling over the flame all at once, instead of one stick at a time. Once the flames lick up through the kindling, place another handful perpendicularly across the first. When this stage is burning well, advance to the next size. Continue crisscrossing your fuel until the largest size is burning and the fire is self-supporting. If you have leftover material, set it aside—in a dry place—so that it can be used to start another fire later. If you have a problem building your fire, reevaluate your heat, oxygen, and fuel to determine which one is not present or is inadequate for success.

SURVIVAL TIPS

CANDLES MAKE A GREAT HEAT AND TINDER SOURCE

Once lit, a candle can provide the heat needed to light tinder, or it can even serve as a fire's tinder. Stay-lit birthday candles are a good option, as are the eight- to ten-hour emergency-survival candles.

NATURAL TINDER THAT BURNS EVEN WHEN WET

Birch bark and pitch wood both have a strong resin that can easily be lit even when wet. I have done experiments with both, placing them underwater for twenty-four hours and then preparing them as any other tinder before attempting to light. In both cases, they easily lit from a spark.

USING SQUAW WOOD

As a general rule, the lower branches on a tree, or squaw wood, are considered dead, not green, when they easily snap away from the trunk. In cold weather, however, live green frozen branches will also snap free from the trunk. To determine whether a branch is dead or green, cut a small section of the bark away. If a meaty cambium layer is present, the branch is green; if not, the branch is dead and would be a great source of fuel for your fire. If wet, remove all lichen and bark, and split the larger branches in half.

7

Signaling

During an average year, the U.S. National Park System has around four thousand search-and-rescue operations. Of these, approximately half of the missions involve a seriously injured or ill subject, and in 5 percent of the cases the victim dies. A properly utilized signal increases a survivor's chances of being rescued. A signal has two purposes: First, it attracts rescuers to your whereabouts; and second, it helps them hone in on your exact location.

SIGNALS THAT ATTRACT RESCUE

The most effective distress signals for attracting attention are aerial flares and parachute flares, because they are moving, spectacular, and cover a large sighting area.

AERIAL FLARE

This signal is a one-time-use item and should be used only if a rescue team, aircraft, or a vessel is sighted. As with all pyrotechnic devices, it is flammable and should be handled with caution. Most aerial flares are fired by pulling a chain. In general, you'll hold the launcher so that the firing end—where the flare comes out—is pointed overhead and skyward, allowing the chain to drop straight down. Make sure the hand holding the launcher is located within the safe area, as detailed on the device you are using. Then, while the flare is pointed skyward, use your free hand to grasp and pull the chain sharply downward. For safe use and best results, hold the flare away from your body and perpendicular to the ground. The average aerial flares will have a 500-foot launch altitude, six-second burn time, and 12,000 candlepower. Under optimal conditions, these flares have been sighted up to 30 miles away. Many aerial flares float and are waterproof, and most have an average size of 1 inch in diameter and about 4½ inches long, when collapsed. Some flares are disposable; others allow replacement cartridges. The Orion Star-Tracer and the SkyBlazer XLT aerial flares are two good examples and can be found in most sporting-goods or marine stores.

PARACHUTE FLARE

A parachute flare is simply an aerial flare attached to a parachute. The parachute allows for a longer burn time while the flare floats down to earth. Like the aerial flare, this signal is a one-time-use item and should be used only if a rescue team, aircraft, or a vessel is sighted. It, too, is flammable and should be handled with caution. The Pains Wessex SOLAS Mark 3 parachute flare can reach a height of 1,000 feet and produce a brilliant 30,000 candlepower. The flare's red light drifts down to earth under a parachute and has a burn time of about forty seconds.

When using an aerial or parachute flare, you need to adjust for any drift from the wind. Since you want the flare to ignite directly overhead, you'll need to point the flare slightly into the wind. Exactly how much you'll need to point it into the wind is hard to determine, but usually 5 to 10 degrees will suffice.

SIGNALS THAT PINPOINT YOUR LOCATION

Once help is on the way, handheld red signal flares, orange smoke signals, signal mirrors, kites, strobe lights, whistles, and ground-to-air signals serve as beacons to help rescuers pinpoint your position and keep them on course.

HANDHELD RED SIGNAL FLARE

This signal is a one-time-use item and should be used only if a rescue team, aircraft, or a vessel is sighted. It is flammable and should be handled with caution. To light one, stand with your back to the wind, and point the flare away from your face and body during and after lighting. Most red signal flares are ignited by removing the cap and striking the ignition button with the cap's abrasive side. To avoid burns, hold the flare in its safe area, and never hold it overhead. Most devices will burn for two minutes, have a candlepower of 500, and are about 1 inch in diameter by 9 inches long. For increased burn time and candlepower, you might consider getting a handheld marine red signal flare, which average a burn time of three minutes and a 700 candlepower.

ORANGE SMOKE SIGNAL

This signal also is a one-time-use item and should be used only if a rescue team, aircraft, or a vessel is sighted. It, too, is flammable and should be handled with caution. To light one, stand with your back to the wind, and point the device away from your face and body during and after its lighting. Other than wind, snow, or rain, the biggest problem associated with a smoke signal is that cold air keeps the smoke close to the ground, sometimes dissipating it before it reaches the heights needed to be seen.

SkyBlazer smoke signal

The SkyBlazer smoke signal is about the size of a 35-millimeter film container and thus is easy to carry. It's easy to use, and the directions are on the container. Simply remove its seal, pull the chain, and then place it on the ground. The signal lasts for only forty-five seconds under optimal

Rick Sexton holding an orange smoke signal.

conditions and produces only a small volume of orange smoke. In order to increase the smoke to a more appropriate level, I have used two at once. *Note:* The SkyBlazer smoke signal is not a handheld device and should be set on the ground once ignited.

Orion handheld orange smoke signal

The Orion signal is bigger than the SkyBlazer. It comes in two sizes: marine and wilderness. The marine signal is about the size of a road flare, and the wilderness signal is half that. The Orion, too, has easy-to-read directions right on the signal. Simply remove the cap, and strike the ignition button with the abrasive part of the cap. To avoid burns, hold the flare in its safe area, and never hold it overhead. These signals put out a lot of smoke and last over sixty seconds. If space permits, this is a far more effective signal than the SkyBlazer. *Note:* Orion also makes a floating orange smoke signal that lasts for four minutes.

SIGNAL MIRROR (WITH SIGHTING HOLE)

On clear, sunny days, signal mirrors have been seen from as far away as 70 to 100 miles. Although the signal mirror is a great signaling device, it requires practice to become proficient in its use. Most signal mirrors have directions on the back, but the following are general guidelines on how

Signal mirror with sighting hole

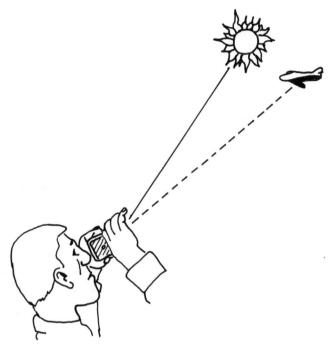

Using a signal mirror

they should be used. Holding the signal mirror between the index finger and thumb of one hand, reflect the sunlight from the mirror onto your other hand. While maintaining the sun's reflection on your free hand, bring the mirror up to eye level and look through the sighting hole. If done properly, you should see a bright white or orange spot of light in the sighting hole. This is commonly called the aim indicator, or fireball. Holding the mirror close to your eye, slowly turn it until the aim indicator is on your intended target. If you lose sight of the aim indicator, start over. *Note:* If signaling an aircraft, stop flashing the pilot after you're certain he's spotted you, as the flash may impede his vision. On land, slightly wiggle the mirror to add movement to the signal. At sea, hold the mirror steady to contrast the sparkles created by the natural movement of the water. Since the mirror can be seen from great distances, sweep the horizon periodically throughout the day, even if no rescue vehicles are in sight. To avoid obstructive shade, be sure to remove your hat when using a signal mirror.

KITE

A kite is a highly visible signal that not only attracts attention to your location, but also helps rescuers pinpoint where you are. David Instrument's Sky-Alert Parafoil Rescue Kite is a good example. The 28-by-38-inch kite flies in 5 to 25 knots of wind and requires only about 8 to 10 knots to lift another signaling device such as a strobe or handheld flare. A benefit of this signal is that it can be working for you while you attend to other needs. In addition to providing a great signal, flying the kite can also help alleviate stress.

STROBE LIGHT

A strobe light is a device that fits in the palm of your hand and provides an ongoing intermittent flash. ACR Electronics Personal Rescue Strobe is a good example of this. It delivers a bright flash (250,000 peak lumens) at one-second intervals and can run up to eight hours on AA batteries. It is visible for up to 1 nautical mile on a clear night. As with all battery-operated devices, strobe lights are vulnerable to cold, moisture, sand, and heat; protect the strobe from these hazards by any means available.

WHISTLE

A whistle will never wear out, and its sound travels farther than the screams of the most desperate survivor. Always carry a whistle on your person. If you become lost or separated, immediately begin blowing your whistle in multiple short bursts. Repeat every three to five minutes. If rescue doesn't appear imminent, go about meeting your other survival needs, stopping periodically throughout the day to blow the whistle. It may alert rescuers to your location, even if you're unaware of their presence. Storm Whistle's Storm Safety Whistle is a good example. Its unique design makes it the loudest whistle you can buy, even when soaking wet. It is made from plastic and has easy-to-grip ridges.

GROUND-TO-AIR PATTERN SIGNAL

A ground-to-air signal is an extremely effective device that allows you to attend to your other needs while continuing to alert potential rescuers of your location. Although you can buy signal panels, I'd suggest purchasing a 3-foot-wide by 18-foot-long piece of lightweight nylon—orange for

Simply Survival students set up a ground-to-air signal.

winter, white for summer. There are three basic signal designs you can construct using the nylon.

V=Need assistance

X=Need medical assistance

↑=Proceed this way

Once you've made the appropriate signal design, stake it out so that it holds its form and doesn't blow away. For optimal effect, follow these guidelines:

Size: The ideal signal will have a ratio of 6:1, with its overall size at least 18 feet long by 3 feet wide.

Contrast: The signal should contrast the surrounding ground cover: orange on snow, white on brown or green.

Angularity: Because nature has no perfect lines, a signal with sharp angles will be more effective.

Shadow: In summer, elevate the signal. In winter, stomp or dig an area around the signal that is approximately 3 feet wide. If the sun is shining, either of these methods will create a shadow, which ultimately increases the signal's size.

Movement: Setting up a flag next to your signal may create enough movement to catch the attention of a rescue party. It is also advisable to suspend a flag high above your shelter so that it can be seen from all directions by potential rescuers.

CELLULAR PHONES

Although a cellular phone is a great thing to have, it's not without limitations and often doesn't work in remote areas. Do not rely on one as your sole signaling and rescue device. Not only are cell phones limited by their service area, but they are also vulnerable to cold, moisture, sand, and heat. You'll need to protect the phone from these hazards by any means available.

IMPROVISED SIGNALS

Many manufactured signals are one-time-use items or are limited by their battery life, and it may be necessary to augment them with an improvised signal. A fire can be as effective as a red flare; an improvised smoke generator works better and lasts longer than an orange smoke signal; an improvised signal mirror can be as useful as a manufactured one; and a ground-to-air signal can be made from materials provided by Mother Nature.

FIRE AS A SIGNAL

During the night, fire is probably the most effective means of signaling available. One large fire will suffice to alert rescuers to your location; don't waste time, energy, and wood building three fires in a distress triangle unless rescue is uncertain. If the ground is covered with snow, build the fire on a snow platform to prevent the snow's moisture from putting out the fire. Prepare the wood or other fuel for ignition prior to use, as described in chapter 6.

SMOKE GENERATOR

Smoke is an effective signal if used on a clear, calm day. If the weather is bad, however, chances are that the smoke will dissipate too quickly to be seen. The rules for a smoke signal are the same as those for a fire signal: You only need one; use a platform in snow environments; and prepare the materials for the signal in advance. To make the smoke contrast against its surroundings, add any of the following materials to your fire:

To contrast snow: Use tires, oil, or fuel to create black smoke.

To contrast darker backgrounds: Use boughs, grass, green leaves, moss, ferns, or even a small amount of water to create white smoke.

In heavy snow or rain, you'll need to set up your smoke generator in advance and protect it from the moisture. To accomplish this, build an elevated platform by driving two 6-foot-long wrist-diameter branches 3 feet into the snow, at a 10- to 20-degree angle to the ground. For best results, insert the branches in a location where the ground has a 10- to 20-degree slope, creating a level foundation for smoke generator. Next, place multiple wrist-diameter branches on top of and perpendicular to the first two, so that they are touching one another. In the center of this newly created surface, build, but don't light, a tepee firelay, using a lot of tinder and kindling in the process. Then construct a log-cabin-style firelay around the tepee, using fuel that is thumb-size and larger. Leave a small, quick-access opening that will allow you to reach the tinder when it comes time to light it. Finally, place a heavy bough covering over the top of the whole thing. The bough covering should be thick enough to protect the underlying structure

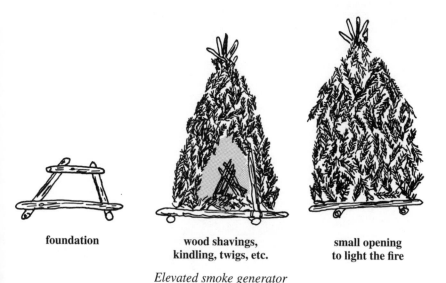

foundation   wood shavings,   small opening
                    kindling, twigs, etc.   to light the fire

Elevated smoke generator

Bill Frye builds the foundation needed for a smoke signal in a snow climate.

Adding a smoke flare to your signal will make it contrast against the snow.

from the snow and rain. When done, the generator should look like a haystack of boughs. Once rescuers have been spotted or appear to be headed in your direction, light the smoke generator, gently picking up and reaching under one side of the boughs. If you should have trouble getting it lit, this is one of the rare circumstances where I'd advise using your red smoke flare as a heat source.

IMPROVISED SIGNAL MIRROR
A signal mirror can be created from anything shiny, such as a metal container, coin, credit card, watch, jewelry, or belt buckle. Although an improvised signal mirror is a great signaling device, it requires practice to become proficient in its use. To use one, follow these steps. Holding the device between the index finger and thumb of one hand, reflect the sunlight from

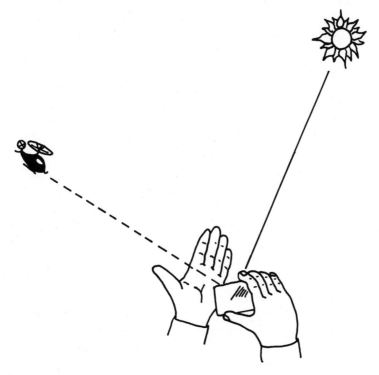

Any shiny reflective material can be used as an improvised signal mirror.

the mirror onto the palm of your other hand. While keeping the reflection on that hand, create a V between your thumb and index finger. Move the light reflection and your hand until the rescue aircraft or other rescuer is in the V. At this point, move the reflected light into the V and onto your intended target. (Also see the note under Signal Mirrors, above.)

IMPROVISED GROUND-TO-AIR PATTERN SIGNAL

If you haven't brought along a signal panel, you can improvise one from whatever Mother Nature provides—boughs, bark, snow, logs, or any other material that contrasts with the ground color. See the guidelines under Ground-to-Air Pattern Signal, above, for basic guidelines of design and construction.

HELICOPTER RESCUE

Helicopter rescues are becoming more frequent as more and more people head into the wilderness. Rescue crews may be civilians, but more often than not, they are either military or Coast Guard. If the helicopter can land, it will. If not, a member of the rescue team will be lowered to your position. At this point, you'll either be hoisted to the helicopter or moved to a better location while in a harness or basket and dangling from the helicopter. Secure all loose items before the helicopter lands, or they may be blown away or sucked up into the rotors. Once the helicopter has landed, do not approach it until signaled to do so, and only approach from the front side. This will ensure that the pilot can see you and decrease your chances of being injured or killed by the rotor blades.

SURVIVAL TIPS

If you become lost or a member of your team is hurt and unable to be moved, stay put: Only depart if the area you are in doesn't meet your needs, rescue is not imminent, and you know how to navigate. If you are lost or stranded in a car, plane, or ATV, stay with it. The vehicle will serve as a ground-to-air signal. When a search is activated, rescuers will begin looking for you in your last known location. If for some reason you need to move, leave a ground-to-air signal pointing in your direction of travel, along with a note telling rescuers of your plans. If you do move, go to high ground, and find a large clearing to signal from.

Properly locate your signal site: Your signal site should be close to your camp or shelter; located in a large clearing that has 360-degree visibility; and free of shadows.

Use one-time-use signals at the right time: Many signals are one-time-use items and thus should be ignited only when you see or hear a potential rescuer and are sure he or she is headed in your direction.

ALWAYS BE PREPARED

Since you never know if someone is nearby, blow your whistle every five to ten minutes, and occasionally scan the horizon with your signal mirror. To avoid watching rescuers disappear while still fumbling with your signal, learn how to use them in advance, and make sure they are ready to use before rescue is near. Since seconds can mean the difference between life and death, don't delay in preparing or establishing a signal.

USING A SPACE BLANKET AS A SIGNAL

A strong, silver-and-orange space blanket can serve as an improvised signal. Silver will contrast with the brown or green color of bare ground, and orange will do the same in a snowy environment. To use as a signal, place the space blanket in a clearing, with the appropriate contrasting side up, and weigh down the edges so it won't blow away. As you meet your other needs, a well-positioned space blanket will alert any potential rescuers to your location. The space blanket should be used as a signal only when not needed to meet other survival needs.

8

Water

Water is far more important than food. You can live anywhere from three weeks to two months without food, but only days without water. Thus you need to pack in enough water for at least one day, along with the necessary equipment to procure more.

Our bodies are composed of approximately 60 percent water. Looking at this in more detail, our brains are composed of about 70 percent water, our blood 82 percent, and our lungs around 90 percent water. In the bloodstream, water helps metabolize and transport the vital elements, carbohydrates, and proteins necessary to fuel our bodies. On the flip side, water helps us dispose of our bodily waste. Water plays a vital role in our ability to get through a day, and it's hard to understand why so many people drink so little.

During a normal, nonstrenuous day, your body needs 2 to 3 quarts of water. When you're physically active or in extreme hot or cold environments, however, that need increases to at least 4 to 6 quarts a day. Cold climates tend to be more problematic than hot climates, since a person normally doesn't sweat or feel the need to drink—until it is almost too late. However, following the general rule of 4 to 6 quarts will usually suffice. When cold, the body loses fluids through the process of warming itself. Drinking enough water is necessary to ward off hypothermia as well as dehydration. A person who's mildly dehydrated will develop excessive thirst and become irritable, weak, and nauseated. As the dehydration worsens, the person will show a decrease in his or her mental capacity and coordination. At this point, it will become difficult to accomplish even the simplest of tasks. The importance of water in a cold environment cannot be overemphasized.

WATER SOURCES AND PROCUREMENT

Since your body needs a constant supply of water, you'll eventually need to procure water from Mother Nature. In a cold-weather environment, snow and ice are often available, but sometimes you'll need to find other sources.

SURFACE WATER

Surface water may be obtained from a pond, lake, river, or stream. This water is usually easy to access, but it is prone to contamination from bacteria, viruses, and protozoans and should always be purified. If using surface water, in most situations you should be able to walk to your water source. (If you build your shelter close to surface water during a rainy season, consider how high it will rise.)

Surface water may not always be easy to access or may not be palatable. If the ground is not frozen solid, you can create a seepage basin well to filter out some of the stagnant flavor and provide ease of access. This filtering process is similar to what happens as groundwater moves toward an aquifer. To create a seepage basin well, dig a 3-foot-wide hole about 10 feet from your water source. Dig it down until water begins to seep in, and then go about another foot. Line the sides with wood or rocks, so that no more mud will fall in, and let it sit overnight. You can use this same process if you're near the ocean by simply digging a hole one dune inland from the beach. As with the other basin wells, dig until you hit water, and then line the sides before letting it sit overnight.

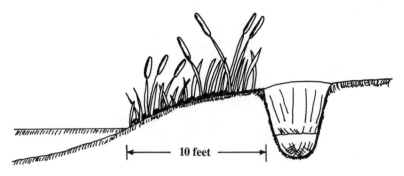

Filtering with a seepage basin well

GROUNDWATER

Groundwater is found under the earth's surface. This water is naturally filtered as it moves through the ground and into underground reservoirs known as aquifers. Although treatment may not be necessary, always err on the side of caution. Groundwater here refers to not only the water that is directly under the surface, but also natural springs where the water rises up to the surface. Locating groundwater is probably the most difficult part of accessing it. Look for things that seem out of place, such as a small area of lush green vegetation at the base of a hill, surrounded by brown vegetation. A marshy area with a fair amount of cattail or hemlock growth may provide a clue that groundwater is available. I have found natural springs in desert areas and running water less than 6 feet below the earth's surface using these clues. For ease of access, you can dig a small well at the source, as described above.

RAINWATER

You can collect rainwater by setting out containers or digging a small hole and lining it with plastic or another nonporous material. After the rain has stopped, look for water in crevasses, fissures, and low-lying areas.

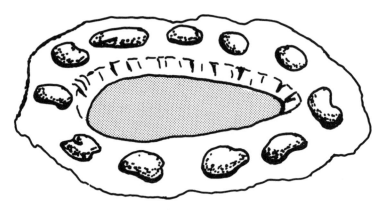

Collecting rainwater

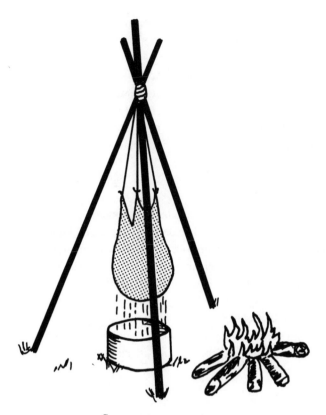

Snow water generator

SNOW OR ICE

Do not eat snow or ice! The energy lost during this process is not equal to the benefit. Melt the snow or ice first, either in a cooking pot suspended over a fire, or by adding it to a partially full canteen and then shaking the container or placing it between the layers of your clothing so that your body's radiant heat will melt the snow or ice. In large groups, a water generator can be created from a tripod and porous material. Create a large pouch by attaching the porous material to the tripod. Fill the pouch with snow or ice, and place the tripod just close enough to the fire to start melting it, but not too close. Use a container to collect the water. This method will provide an ongoing large and quick supply of water. The biggest draw-back is that the water will taste a little like smoke. If the sun is out, you could melt the snow or ice by digging a cone-shaped hole, lining it with a tarp or similar nonporous material, and placing snow or ice on the material at the top of the hole. As it melts, the resulting water will collect at the bottom. Don't use sea ice unless it's virtually free of the salts found in sea-water. Sea ice that has rounded corners, shatters easily, and is bluish or black is usually safe to use. When in doubt, do a taste test. If it tastes salty, don't use it.

DEW

Although dew does not provide a large volume of water, it should not be overlooked. Dew will accumulate on grass, leaves, rocks, and equipment at dawn and dusk and should be collected at those times, since it will quickly freeze or evaporate. Use any porous material to absorb the dew, then wring the moisture out of the cloth and into your mouth.

WATER INDICATORS

If snow and ice are not present, understanding water indicators created by birds, mammals, and the terrain will be helpful when trying to find water.

BIRDS

Birds frequently fly toward water at dawn and dusk in a direct, low flight path. This is especially true of birds that feed on grain, such as pigeons and finches. Flesh-eating birds can also be seen exhibiting this flight pattern, but their need for water isn't as great, and they don't require as many trips to the water source. Birds observed circling high in the air during the day are often doing it over water, as well.

MAMMALS

Like birds, mammals frequently visit watering holes at dawn and dusk. This is especially true of mammals that eat a grain or grassy type of diet. Watching their travel patterns or evaluating mammal trails may help you find a water source. Trails that merge into one are usually a good pointer, and following the merged trail often leads to water.

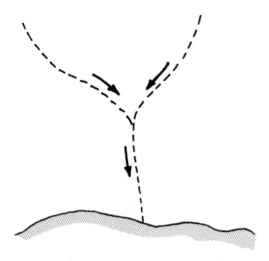

Two trails merging into one often point towards water.

LAND FEATURES

Drainages and valleys are good water indicators, as are winding trails of deciduous trees. Plush green vegetation found at the base of a cliff or mountain may indicate a natural spring or underground source of water.

NATURAL WATER FILTRATION

Filtration systems do not purify water! At best, they remove unwanted particles and make the water more palatable. A seepage basin is one method of filtering water. It may not always, however, take away the water's awful taste. Another method is to use a layered filtering device that employs grass, sand, and charcoal. Running water through grass, sand, and black charcoal does more than just remove unwanted particles; it also makes the water taste better. This system can be created using a three-tiered tripod design or by simply layering the materials inside a container that allows the water passage, such as a large coffee can. For a three-tiered tripod, tie three sections of porous material (such as a handkerchief) about 1 foot apart, and fill one each with grass, sand, and charcoal, from top to bottom. To use, simply pour the water into the top, and catch it in a container as it departs the bottom section.

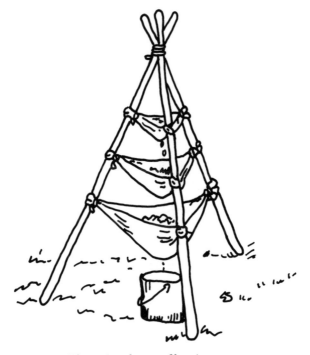

Three-tiered water filtration system

WATER IMPURITIES

According to the Centers for Disease Control (CDC), water contaminated with microorganisms will cause over a million illnesses and one thousand deaths in the United States each year. The primary disease-causing organisms, or pathogens, fall into three categories: protozoans (including cysts), bacteria, and viruses.

PROTOZOANS

Protozoans are one-celled organisms that vary in size from 2 to 100 microns, live in many insects and animals, and survive in cysts (protective shells) when outside of an organism. They include *Giardia* and *Cryptosporidium.* It only takes a few of these organisms to infect someone, and once inside a host, protozoans will rapidly reproduce, causing severe diarrhea, abdominal cramps, bloating, fatigue, and weight loss.

BACTERIA

Bacteria can be as tiny as 0.2 microns, much smaller than protozoans. Some examples are typhoid, paratyphoid, dysentery, and cholera. Bacteria are often present in both wild and domestic animals. Once in the water, it can survive for weeks, even longer if frozen in ice.

VIRUSES

Viruses can be as small as 0.004 microns, which makes it easy for them to pass through a filter. Viruses found in water include hepatitis A and E, Norwalk virus, rotavirus, echovirus, and poliovirus. Unlike protozoans and bacteria, there is no treatment for a waterborne viral infection, and this makes them a significant health risk, especially for people who have a compromised immune system.

PURIFYING WATER

There are three basic methods for treating your water: commercial filtration systems, boiling, and chemicals treatments.

COMMERCIAL PURIFYING SYSTEMS

A filter is not a purifying system. In general, filters remove protozoans; microfilters remove protozoans and bacteria; and purifiers remove protozoans, bacteria, and viruses. A purifier is simply a microfilter with an iodine and a carbon element added. The iodine kills viruses, and the carbon element removes the iodine taste and reduces the presence of organic chemical contaminants, such as pesticides, herbicides, and chlorine, as well as heavy metals. Unlike filters, purifiers must be registered with the EPA to demonstrate effectiveness against waterborne pathogens, including cysts, bacteria, and viruses. A purifier costs more than a filter. You'll need to decide what level of risk you are willing to take, as waterborne viruses are becoming more and more prominent. On the downside, a purifier tends to clog more quickly than most filters. To increase the longevity of your system, use the following guidelines (in no way should they supersede your manufacturer's recommendations).

Clean, scrub, and disinfect the filter after each use, according to the manufacturer's guidelines. *Note:* Some filters should not be scrubbed, and some are self-cleaning.

If at all possible, procure clean water, such as that found in a creek's pools or similar areas. To avoid sand, mud, and debris, keep the suction hose away from the water's bottom; this may require a foam float.

If muddy water is your only choice, fill a clean container with the muddy water, and let it sit for several hours (overnight, if time permits) or until the sediment has settled to the bottom of the container. Another option would be to first run the water through an improvised filter, as described above.

Backwash the filter according to the manufacturer's recommended schedule. This process helps remove any accumulated debris from the system.

Since a purifying system can freeze, expand, and crack in subfreezing temperatures, protect it as much as possible.

Purifiers come in a pump style or a ready-to-drink bottle design.

Pump purifiers

Probably the best-known pump purifiers are made by PUR Explorer, which is an ideal system for the wilderness traveler. As a purifying system, it protects against protozoans, bacteria, and viruses. The Explorer is an easy-to-use, high-output, self-cleaning system that weighs 20 ounces. Its 0.3-micron filtering cartridge can produce up to 1.5 liters of water per minute and under normal conditions will not need to be replaced until it has provided around 100 gallons (400 liters) of drinkable water. Follow the manufacturer's guidelines for maintenance of your pump filter.

Bottle purifiers

Probably the best-known bottle filter is the 34-ounce Exstream Mackenzie, an ideal system for the wilderness traveler. As a purifying system, it protects against protozoans, bacteria, and viruses. The benefit of a bottle purifier is its ease of use—simply fill the bottle with water and start drinking, following the manufacturer's directions. It requires no assembly or extra space in your pack. On the downside, it filters only about 26 gallons (100 liters) before you'll need to replace the cartridge, and unless you carry several, you'll need to be in an area with multiple water sources throughout

PUR water purification system

your travel. Maintenance of these systems is simple. When not in use, allow the cartridge to completely dry before storing; before resuming use, flush the system several times with tap water.

When commercial purification systems are not available, another option would be to boil or chemically treat the water.

BOILING

To kill any disease-causing microorganisms that might be in your water, the Environmental Protection Agency (EPA) advocates using a vigorous boil for one minute. My rational mind tells me that this must be based on science and should work. After seeing one of my friends lose about 40 pounds from a severe case of giardiasis, however, I almost always boil it longer. You decide what is right for you.

CHEMICAL TREATMENT
When unable to boil your water, you may elect to use chlorine or iodine. These chemicals are effective against bacteria, viruses, and *Giardia,* but according to the EPA, there is some question about their ability to protect you against *Cryptosporidium.* In fact, the EPA advises against using chemicals to purify surface water. Once again, it's up to you. Chlorine is preferred over iodine, since it seems to offer better protection against *Giardia.* Combining a chemical treatment with a commercial filtering device will make your water safe to drink. Both chlorine and iodine tend to be less effective in cold water.

Chlorine
The amount of chlorine to use for purifying water depends on the amount of available chlorine in the solution, which can usually be found on the label.

Available Chlorine	Drops per Quart of Clear Water
1%	10 drops
4–6 %	2 drops
7–10 %	1 drop
unknown	10 drops

If the water is cloudy or colored, double the normal amount of chlorine required for the percentage used. Add the chlorine to the water in a lidded container, wait three minutes, and then vigorously shake the water, with the lid slightly loose, allowing some water to seep out. Then seal the lid on the container and wait another twenty-five to thirty minutes before loosening the lid and shaking again. At this point, consider the water safe to consume, provided there is no *Cryptosporidium* in the water.

Iodine
There are two forms of iodine that are commonly used to treat water: tincture and tablets. The tincture is nothing more than the common household iodine that you may have in your medical kit. This product is usually a 2 percent iodine solution, and you'll need to add five drops to each quart of water. For cloudy water, double this amount. The treated water should be mixed

and allowed to stand for thirty minutes before use. With iodine tablets, use one tablet per quart of water if it is warm, and two tablets per quart if the water is cold or cloudy. Each bottle of iodine tablets should have the particulars of how it should be mixed and how long you should wait before drinking the water. If no directions are available, add the tablets to the water in a lidded container, wait three minutes, and then vigorously shake the water with the lid slightly loose, allowing some water to seep out. Then seal the lid on the container and wait another twenty-five to thirty minutes before loosening the lid and shaking again. At this point, consider the water safe to consume, provided the water does not contain *Cryptosporidium.*

DISPELLING MYTHS ABOUT WATER

NEVER DRINK URINE!

By the time you even think about doing this, you are very dehydrated. That means your urine is full of salts and other waste products. For a hydrated person, urine is 95% water and the rest is waste products like urea, uric acid, and salts. As you become dehydrated, the amount of water decreases, and the concentration of salts increases substantially. If you drink these salts, the body will draw upon its water reserves to help eliminate them, and thus you will actually lose more water than you might gain from your urine.

NEVER DRINK SALT WATER!

Saltwater concentrations are often higher than those found in urine. As with urine, if you drink saltwater, the body will draw upon its water reserves to help eliminate the salt, and thus you will actually lose more water than you gain.

NEVER DRINK BLOOD!

Blood is composed of plasma (predominantly water and salts), red blood cells, white blood cells, and platelets. Plasma composes about 55 percent of the blood's volume, and in addition to water and salts, it also carries a large number of important proteins (albumin, gamma globulin, and clotting factors) and small molecules (vitamins, minerals, nutrients, and waste products). Waste products produced during metabolism, such as urea and

uric acid, are carried by the blood to the kidneys, where they are trans-
ferred from the blood into urine and eliminated from the body. The kidneys
carefully maintain the salt concentration in plasma. If you drink blood, you
are basically ingesting salts and proteins, and the body will draw upon its
water reserves to help eliminate them, and thus you will actually lose more
water than you might gain.

SURVIVAL TIPS

OTHER WATER YOU SHOULD AVOID:
Avoid collecting water from areas with oily films or slicks, significant algae
overgrowth, or where dead animals are located. If this is your only water
source, you may decide to dig a natural filtration system in the ground close
by as a means of collecting this water, or perhaps pour it through a three-
tiered filter prior to treating and drinking it.

PREVENTING WATER FROM FREEZING AT NIGHT:
Dig a snow refrigerator, with a 12-inch wall all the way around (including
the door), and place your water container in it so that the lid is facing down.
If the lid were up and did not have water contact, its chances of freezing shut
would greatly increase. *Note:* Nonlubricated condoms can be used to store
water; however, you'll need to place them inside a sock or other item for
added strength and support.

9

Food

The body works hard in cold climates, keeping warm and meeting your needs often under less-than-favorable conditions. The ideal diet includes foods that contain all five of these basic elements:

1. Carbohydrates: Easily digested food elements that provide rapid energy. Most often found in fruits, vegetables, and whole grains.
2. Protein: Helps with the building of body cells. Most often found in fish, meat, poultry, and blood.
3. Fats: Slowly digested food elements that provide long-lasting energy, which is normally utilized once the carbohydrates are gone. Most often found in butter, cheese, oils, nuts, eggs, and animal fats. In cold environments, the natives often eat fats before bed, believing it will help keep them warm throughout the night.
4. Vitamins: Provide no calories but aid in the body's daily function and growth. Vitamins occur in most foods, and when you maintain a well-balanced diet, you will rarely become depleted.
5. Minerals: Provide no calories but aid with building and repairing the skeletal system and regulating the body's normal growth. Like vitamins, these are obtained when a well-balanced diet is followed. Minerals also are often present in water.

In harsh, cold-weather conditions, your diet should average between 4,500 and 5,000 calories a day, consisting of approximately 50 to 70 percent carbohydrates, 20 to 30 percent proteins, and 20 to 30 percent fats. The time required to convert carbohydrates, proteins, and fats into simple sugars increases—in that order—due to the complexity of the molecule.

Steaming oatmeal

FOODS TO PACK

If backpacking, weight will be an issue. To compensate, take dry foods like cereal, pasta, rice, wheat, and oatmeal, or purchase freeze-dried meals, which are a great option but tend to be expensive.

BREAKFAST

Cooked oatmeal or similar cereal, combined with dried fruit and rehydrated milk, is a great start to the day.

LUNCH

Lunch is actually a constant snack that should be consumed in small quantities and frequently throughout the day. Gorp (nuts, candy, raisins, and dehydrated fruits), granola (grains mixed with honey or sugar and combined with dehydrated fruit and nuts), fruit leather, and pemmican are great lunch options.

DINNER

For dinner, consider prepackaged meals like mixed rice, ramen noodles, macaroni, or freeze-dried meals. To increase the value of the dinner meal, you may want to add a dried meat (chicken, beef, or fish), freeze-dried vegetable or fruit, or a dehydrated soup mixture.

BEDTIME SNACK
Just before bed, eat a small protein meal. As the body breaks down the protein, it will produce heat, which will aid in keeping you warm through the night.

As long as you have planned out the food for your trip properly and nothing goes wrong, you'll never need to look for food elsewhere. Should you find yourself short, however, or perhaps in a survival situation, you may need to look to Mother Nature to replenish your supply.

PLANTS
Plants can provide a major source of your diet. The best way to learn whether a plant is edible—or not—is from those who are native to the area, along with a good plant reference book. Always be careful, and always positively

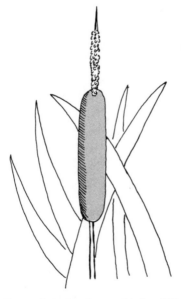

Cattail is a plant that has multiple edible sections.

identify a plant before eating it. If you don't have any references and need to establish the edibility of a plant, then use the universal edibility test; this should only be used under the most extreme conditions, when long-term survival is at stake.

UNIVERSAL EDIBILITY TEST

General rules of the edibility test
1. Ensure that there's an abundant supply of the plant.
2. Use only fresh vegetation.
3. Always wash your plants with treated water.
4. Only perform the test on one plant or plant part at a time.
5. During the test, don't consume anything else other than purified water.
6. Don't eat eight hours prior to starting the test.

Identifying characteristics of plants to avoid (general guidelines; there are exceptions)
1. Mushrooms or mushroomlike appearance.
2. Umbrella-shaped flower clusters (resembling parsley, parsnip, or dill).
3. Plants with milky sap or sap that turns black when exposed to the air.
4. Bulbs (resembling an onion or garlic).
5. Carrotlike leaves, roots, or tubers.
6. Bean- or pealike appearance.
7. Plants with fungal infection (common in spoiled plants procured off the ground).
8. Plants with shiny leaves or fine hairs.

To test a plant
1. Break the plant into its basic components: leaves, stems, roots, buds, and flowers.
2. Test only one part of the potential food source at a time.
3. Smell the plant for strong or acidlike odors. If present, it may be best to select another plant.
4. Prepare the plant part in the fashion in which you intend to consume it (raw, boiled, baked).

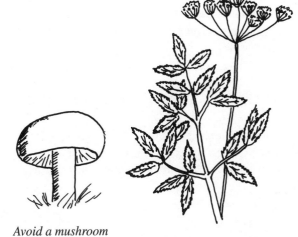

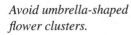

*Avoid a mushroom
or mushroomlike
appearance.*

*Avoid umbrella-shaped
flower clusters.*

*Avoid bulbs resembling
onions or garlic.*

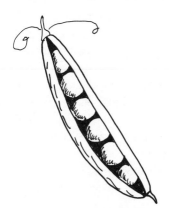

*Avoid carrotlike
leaves, roots, or tubers.*

*Avoid a bean- and
pealike appearance.*

*Avoid plants with shiny
leaves or fine hairs.*

5. Place a piece of the plant part being tested on the inside of your wrist for fifteen minutes. Monitor for burning, stinging, or irritation. If any of these occur, discontinue the test, select another plant or another component of the plant, and start over.

6. Hold a small portion, about a teaspoonful, of the plant to your lips and monitor for five minutes. If any burning or irritation occurs, discontinue the test, select another plant or another component of the plant, and start over.

7. Place the plant on your tongue, holding it there for fifteen minutes. Do not swallow any of the plant juices. If any burning or irritation occurs, discontinue the test, select another plant or another component of the plant, and start over.

8. Thoroughly chew the teaspoonful of the plant part for fifteen minutes. Do not swallow any of the plant or its juices. If you experience a reaction, discontinue the test, select another plant or another component of the plant, and start over. If there is no burning, stinging, or irritation, swallow the plant.

9. Wait eight hours. Monitor for cramps, nausea, vomiting, or other abdominal irritations. If any occur, induce vomiting and drink plenty of water. If you do experience a reaction, discontinue the test, select another plant or another component of the plant, and start over.

10. If no problems are experienced, eat ½ cup of the plant, prepared in the same fashion as before. Wait another eight hours. If no ill effects occur, the plant part is edible when prepared in the same fashion as tested.

11. Test all parts of the plant you intend to use before consumption. Some plants have both edible and poisonous portions. Do not assume that a part that is edible when cooked is edible when raw, or vice versa. Always eat the plant in the same fashion in which the edibility test was performed on it.

12. After the plant is determined to be edible, eat it in moderation. Although considered safe, large amounts may cause cramps and diarrhea.

THE BERRY RULE

In general, the edibility of berries can be classified according to their color and composition. The following are approximate guidelines to help you

Aggregate berries are 99% edible.

determine if a berry is poisonous. In no way should the berry rule replace the edibility test. Use it as a general guide to determine whether the edibility test needs to be performed upon the berry. The only berries that should be eaten without testing are those that you can positively identify as nonpoisonous.

1. Green, yellow, and white berries are 10 percent edible.
2. Red berries are 50 percent edible.
3. Purple, blue, and black berries are 90 percent edible.
4. Aggregate berries, such as thimbleberries, raspberries, and blackberries, are considered 99 percent edible.

EDIBLE PARTS OF A PLANT
Some plants are completely edible, whereas others have both edible and poisonous parts. *Unless you have performed the edibility test on the whole plant, eat only the parts that you know are edible.* A plant can be broken down into several distinct components: underground, stems and leaves, flowers, fruits, nuts, seeds and grains, and gums, resins, and saps.

Underground (tubers, roots and rootstalks, and bulbs)

Found underground, these plant parts have a high degree of starch and are best served baked or boiled. Some examples of these are potatoes (tuber), cattail (root and rootstalk), and wild onion (bulbs).

Stems and leaves (shoots and stems, leaves, pith, and cambium)

Plants that produce stems and leaves are probably the most abundant source of edible vegetation in the world. Their high vitamin content makes them a valuable component to our daily diet. *Shoots* grow like asparagus and are best when parboiled: boiled five minutes, drained off, and boiled again until done. Some edible examples of these are bracken fern (only to be eaten in moderation), young bamboo, and cattail. *Leaves* may be eaten raw or cooked, but to achieve the highest nutritional value, they are best eaten raw. Dock, plantain, amaranth, and sorrel are a few examples of edible leaves. *Pith,* found inside the stem of some plants, is often very high in food value. Some edible examples are sago, rattan, coconut, and sugar. *Cambium* is the inner bark found between the bark and the wood of a tree. It can be eaten raw, cooked, or dried and then pulverized into flour.

Flowers (flowers, buds, and pollen)

Flowers, buds, and pollen are high in food value and are served best when eaten raw or in a salad. Some edible examples include hibiscus (flower), rose hips (buds), and cattail (pollen).

Fruits (sweet and nonsweet)

Fruits are the seed-bearing parts of plants and can be found in all areas of the world. They are best when eaten raw, as they retain all of their nutritional value, but they may also be cooked. Examples of sweet fruits are apples, prickly pears, huckleberries, and wild strawberries. Examples of nonsweet fruits include tomatoes, cucumbers, plantains, and horseradish.

Nuts

Nuts are high in fat and protein and can be found around the world. Most can be eaten raw, but some, like acorns, require leaching with several changes of water to remove their tannic acid content.

Seeds and Grains

The seeds and grains of many fruits are a valuable food resource and should not be overlooked. Some examples are grasses and millet. These are best eaten when ground into flour or roasted.

Gums and Resins

Gums and resins are sap that collects on the outside of trees and plants. Their high nutritional value makes them a great augment to any meal. Examples can be found on pine and maple trees.

ARCTIC PLANTS

Plants in an arctic area are normally small and stunted, due to the long-term effects of permafrost, low temperatures, and a short growing season. In the *open tundra,* a wide range of edible plants are available. During summer months, you can find Labrador tea, fireweed, dwarf arctic birch, willow, and an abundance of various other plants and berries. During winter months, you'll find roots, rootstalks, and frozen berries under the snow. Lichens can be found year-round, but be sure you can identify them and that you prepare them correctly, as some can be poisonous (see below). In *bog or swamp regions,* water sedge, cattail, dwarf birch, and berries are available. In *wooded areas,* trees such as birch, spruce, poplar, and aspen, along with many berry-producing plants, such as huckleberries, cranberries, raspberries, cloudberries, and crowberries, can be found. In addition, wild rose hips, Labrador tea, alder, and various other shrubs are very abundant. In cold environments, spruce, birch, and lichens are often the only available vegetation.

Spruce

Spruce, both black and white, is a common northern evergreen. It has short, stiff singular needles and cones that are small with thin scales. The resinous-flavored buds, needles, and stems are rich sources of vitamin C when eaten raw. The inner bark can be collected in the spring and early summer and eaten raw or dried and pounded into flour for later use.

Dwarf arctic birch

Dwarf arctic birch is a shrub that has thin, tooth-edged leaves and bark that can be peeled off in sheets. The fresh buds and leaves can be eaten raw and are rich sources of vitamin C. The inner bark can be collected in the spring and early summer and eaten raw or dried and pounded into flour for later use. A young shoot of dwarf arctic birch is edible, as are its roots, and both can be eaten raw or cooked.

Lichens

Lichens can be found in almost all cold-weather climates, and most species are edible. Some examples include Iceland moss, peat moss, reindeer lichen, and beard lichen. Beard lichen, which grows on trees, may contain a bitter acid that causes stomach and intestinal irritation. However, if it is boiled, dried, and powdered, the acid is removed, and the powder can be used as flour.

BUGS

Many cultures around the world eat bugs as part of their routine diet. An example of this is pan-fried locusts, considered a delicacy in Algeria. Our phobia about eating bugs is unfortunate, since they provide ample amounts of protein, fats, carbohydrates, calcium, and iron. In addition, when comparing bugs to cattle, sheep, pigs, and chickens they are far more cost effective to raise and have far fewer harmful effects related to their rearing. Although bugs are not harvested for food in the United States, those of us who purchase our foods at the store are eating them every day. The FDA allows certain levels of bugs to be present in various foods. The accepted standards are for up to sixty aphids in 3½ ounces of broccoli, two or three fruitfly maggots in 200 grams of tomato juice, one hundred insect fragments in 25 grams of curry powder, seventy-four mites in 100 grams of

Insects can provide a great source of protein, carbohydrates, and fat.

canned mushrooms, thirteen insect heads in 100 grams of fig paste, and thirty-four fruitfly eggs in a cup of raisins.

A study done by Jared Ostrem and John VanDyk for the entomology department of Iowa State University, comparing the nutritional value of various bugs to that of lean ground beef and fish, showed the following results:

	protein (g)	fats (g)	carbohydrates (g)	calcium (mg)	iron (mg)
crickets	12.9	5.5	5.1	75.8	9.5
small grasshoppers	20.6	6.1	3.9	35.2	5
giant water beetles	19.8	8.3	2.1	43.5	13.6
red ants	13.9	3.5	2.9	47.8	5.7
silkworm pupae	9.6	5.6	2.3	41.7	1.8
termites	14.2	N/A	N/A	0.050	35.5
weevils	6.7	N/A	N/A	0.186	13.1
lean ground beef	24.0	18.3	0	9.0	2.09
fish (broiled cod)	22.95	0.86	0	0.031	1.0

Bugs can be found throughout the world, and they are easy to procure. In addition, the larvae and grubs of many are edible and can be easily found in rotten logs, underground, or under the bark of dead trees. Although a fair number of bugs can be eaten raw, it is best to cook them in order to avoid the ingestion of unwanted parasites. As a general rule, avoid bugs that carry disease (flies, mosquitoes, and ticks), poisonous insects (centipedes and spiders), and bugs that have fine hair, bright colors, and eight or more legs.

CRUSTACEANS

Freshwater and saltwater crabs, crayfish, lobsters, shrimp, and prawns are all forms of crustaceans. Although all are edible, it is important to cook freshwater crustaceans, as many carry parasites.

FRESHWATER CRABS AND CRAYFISH

Freshwater crabs and crayfish are found on moss beds and under rocks and brush at the bottom of streams or swimming in the stream's shallow water.

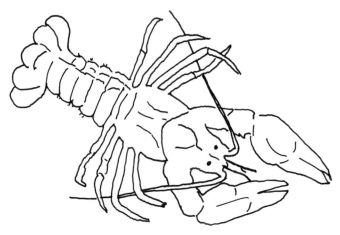

Crustaceans should be cooked because they may carry parasites.

Since they are nocturnal, they are easier to spot at night and then catch by hand or with a scoop net. To catch during the day, use a lobster trap or baited hook. An improvised lobster trap can be made by securely attaching bait to the inside bottom of a container (improvised or not) the size of a large coffee can. If using a can, puncture small holes into the bottom so that water can pass through. Attach enough line to the trap's sides so that it can be lowered and raised from the stream's bottom. Check the trap often. When pulling the container from the water, do it swiftly, but with enough control to avoid pouring your dinner out.

SALTWATER CRAYFISH AND LOBSTERS
Saltwater crayfish and lobsters are found on the ocean bottoms in 10 to 30 feet of water. These crustaceans behave similarly to freshwater crabs and crayfish and can be procured using the same techniques.

FRESHWATER SHRIMP
Freshwater shrimp are abundant in most tropical streams, especially where the water is sluggish. They can be seen swimming or clinging to branches and are easily procured by using either a scoop net or your hand.

SALTWATER SHRIMP

Saltwater shrimp live on or near the sea bottom. Since these shrimp are attracted to light, it's best to hunt them during a full moon or to lure them to the water's surface with a flashlight. Once spotted, simply scoop them up with a net or pluck them from the water with your hand.

MOLLUSKS

If you are located near water, mollusks can provide an almost never-ending food source. However, they should be avoided from April to October. During this time, they accumulate certain poisons that can be harmful to humans. Also avoid marine shellfish that are not covered by water at high tide. The most common types of mollusks are freshwater and saltwater shellfish: bivalves—those with two shells, such as clams, oysters, scallops, and mussels—as well as river and sea snails, freshwater periwinkles, limpets, and chitons. All can be boiled, steamed, or baked.

FRESHWATER MOLLUSKS

Freshwater mollusks include some bivalves, river snails, and periwinkles and are easily procured. Bivalves are found worldwide under all water conditions. River snails and freshwater periwinkles are most plentiful in the rivers, streams, and lakes of the northern coniferous forests.

SALTWATER MOLLUSKS

Mussels, chitons, sea snails, and limpets are all saltwater mollusks and are easily procured at low tide. All can be found in dense colonies on rocks and logs above the surf line.

Avoid mollusks from April to October.

FISH

The best time to fish is just before dawn or just after dusk, at night when the moon is full, and when bad weather is imminent. Fish tend to be close to banks and shallow water in the morning and evening hours. In addition, fish can be found in calm, deep pools, especially where transitions from ripples to calm or calm to ripples occur; under outcroppings and overhanging undercuts, brush, or logs; in eddies below rocks or logs; and at the mouth of an intersection with another stream. Some methods of fish procurement include fishing tackle, gill nets, spears, poisons, and even your bare hands. Ice fishing is possible after freezing has occurred. Since fish tend to congregate in deep water during cold weather, cut a hole in the ice over the estimated deepest point, and drop in your line. Pay close attention to ice stability— don't take any risks that may precipitate your falling through the ice. Avoid fish with a slimy body, bad odor, suspicious color (gills should be pink and scales pronounced), or flesh that remains indented after being pressed on.

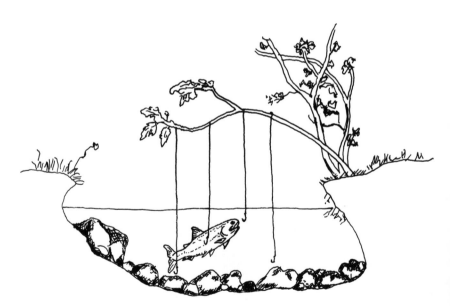

Fish can be found in most cold climates.

FISHING TACKLE

The world is covered with water, and fish as a food source should not be overlooked. If you have fishing tackle, use it. If you don't, you'll need to improvise. Crude tackle isn't very useful for catching small fish like trout, but it is more effective with larger fish like carp, catfish, and whitefish.

Hooks and lines

Hooks are best made from bone or wood, and the ideal material for improvised fishing line is stinging nettle, milkweed, or dogbane, braided into a 10-foot section. Sinew is another option, but when it gets wet, it tends to stretch and its knots loosen. The three most commonly improvised hooks are the skewer hook, cross hook, and barbed thorn or branch hook.

Skewer hook

A skewer hook is a sliver of bone or wood that is notched and tied at the middle. When baited, this hook is turned parallel to the line, making it easier for the fish to swallow. Once the fish takes the bait, a simple tug on the line will turn the skewer sideways, lodging it in the fish's mouth.

Cross hook

A cross hook is made by attaching a crosspiece to a main shank, so that when the bait is applied, the two pieces are parallel to one another. When the fish swallows the hook, a gentle tug on the line will set it by causing the crosspiece to angle out.

Barbed thorn or branch hook

A barbed thorn or branch hook requires minimal effort to create. Using a thorn or branch with a hooklike fork, simply cut a circular notch on one end for the line and sharpen the other.

Attaching the hook

To attach your hook to your braided line, use the following method:

1. Notch the hook shank either at its center or at the distal end, depending on the type of hook you are using.

Three improvised fish hooks

2. Smear it with pitch or other gluelike substance.
3. Wrap and tie your improvised line tightly around the notch.
4. Seal the line and notch area with additional pitch.

Although you could attach a single hook and line to a single pole, I'd advise setting out multiple lines. This method allows you to catch fish while attending to other chores. The goal is to return and find a fish attached to the end of each line.

Gill net
The gill net is very effective and will work for you while you attend to other needs. If you have parachute cord or a similar material, its inner core provides an ideal material for making a net. Other options are braided stinging nettle, milkweed, or dogbane line. In order for the net to stay clear of debris, it should be placed at a slight angle to the current, using stones to anchor the bottom and wood to help the top float. Follow these steps to make a gill net:

1. Tie a piece of line between two trees at eye height. The bigger the net you want, the farther apart the trees should be.
2. Using a girth hitch, tie the center of your inner core line or other material to the upper cord. Use an even number of lines. Space the lines at a distance equal to the width you desire for your net's mesh. For creeks and small rivers, 1 inch is about right.
3. No matter which side you start on, skip the line closest to the tree. Tie the second and third together with an overhand knot, and continue on

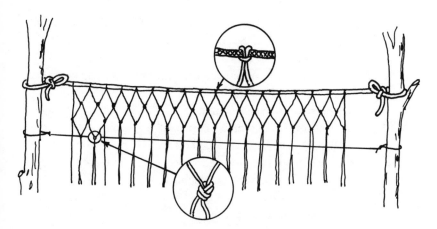

Constructing a gill net

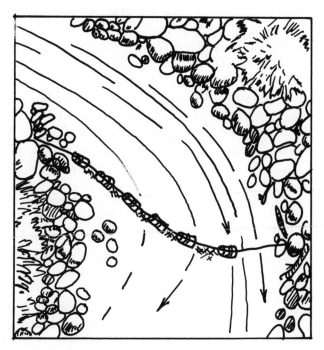

Gill net placement in a creek

down the line, tying together the fourth and fifth, sixth and seventh, and so on. When you reach the end, there should be one line left.

4. Moving in the opposite direction, tie the first line to the second, third to the fourth, and so on. When you reach the end, there shouldn't be any lines left.

5. Repeat the previous two steps until done.

6. If you are concerned about the mesh size, tie a guideline between the two trees. For a 1-inch mesh, tie the line 1 inch below the top, and use it to determine where the overhand knots should be placed. Once a line is completed, move it down another inch, and so on.

7. When done, run parachute line or other material along the net's sides and bottom to help stabilize it.

Scoop net

To make a scoop net, bend the two ends of a 6-foot sapling together to form a circle. You can also use a forked branch by forming a circle with the forked ends. Allow some extra length for a handle. Lash the ends together. The net's mesh can be made in the same method as described for building a gill net, by tying the initial girth hitch to the sapling. Once you have the appropriate size, tie all the lines together using an overhand knot, and trim off any excess line. A scoop net should be used in shallow water or a similar area where fish are visible. Because you'll need to compensate for light refraction below the water, first place the net into the water to obtain the proper alignment. Next, slowly move the net as close to the fish as possible, and allow the fish to become accustomed to it. When ready, scoop the fish up and out of the stream.

Spear

To make a straight spear, procure a long, straight sapling, and sharpen one end to a barbed point. If practical, fire-harden the tip to make it more durable by holding it a few inches above a hot bed of coals until it is brown. To make a forked spear, procure a long, straight sapling and fire-harden the tip. Snugly lash a line around the stick 6 to 8 inches down from one end. Using a knife, split the wood down the center to the lash. To keep the two halves apart, lash a small wedge between them. Sharpen the two prongs into inward-pointing barbs.

Wooden forked spear

A throwing spear should be 5 to 6 feet long. To throw a spear, hold it in your right hand (if left-handed, reverse these instructions), and raise it above your shoulder so that the spear is parallel to the ground. Position your hand at the spear's center point of balance. Place your body so that your left foot is forward and your trunk is perpendicular to the target. Point your left arm and hand toward your target to help guide you when throwing the spear. Once positioned, thrust your right arm forward and release the spear. If you're trying to spear an animal, release the spear at the moment that will best enable you to strike it in the chest or heart.

When using a spear to procure fish, you'll need to compensate for light refraction below the water's surface. In order to obtain proper alignment, place the spear tip into the water before aiming. Moving the spear tip slowly will allow the fish to get accustomed to it until you are ready. Once you have speared a fish, hold it down against the bottom of the stream until you can get your hand between it and the tip of the spear.

Fish traps
Fish traps would perhaps be better called corrals, since the idea is to herd fish into the fenced enclosure. The opening is designed like a funnel, with the narrow end emptying into a cage.

When building these traps in ocean water, select your location during high tide and construct the trap during low tide. On rocky shores, use natural rock pools; on coral islands, use the natural pools that form on the reefs; and on sandy shores, create a dam on the lee side of the offshore sandbar. If you can, block all the openings before the tide recedes. Once the tide goes back out, you can use either a scoop net or a spear to bring your dinner ashore.

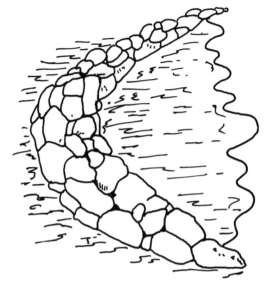

Offshore fish trap

Placement of a fish trap in a creek

In creeks and small rivers, use saplings to create the trap and its funnel. The opening should be on the upstream side so the current will aid in the funneling process. To herd the fish into your trap, start upstream and wade down toward your corral. Once there, close its opening, and use a scoop net or a spear to get the fish out.

PREPARING FISH

To prevent spoilage, prepare the fish as soon as possible. Always do this well away from your shelter. Gut the fish by cutting up its abdomen and then removing the intestines and large blood vessels that lie next to the backbone. Remove the gills and, when applicable, scale and/or skin the fish. On bigger fish, you may want to fillet the meat off the bone. To do this, cut behind the fish's gill plates on each side of its head, and slide the knife under the meat next to the backbone. Keeping the knife firmly placed against the backbone, begin slicing toward the tail. Then, holding the tail's skin, slide the knife between the skin and the meat, cutting forward with a slight sawing motion.

BIRDS

Almost all birds are edible. If nests are nearby, eggs may also be available for consumption. Birds are commonly found at the edge of the woods where clearings end and forests begin, on the banks of rivers and streams, and on lakeshores and seashores. During the warm months in colder climates, birds and waterfowl are abundant. These may include ducks, geese, terns, gulls, owls, and ptarmigan. Young birds are easy to procure with snares, with a baited hook, or, on occasion, by clubbing.

PREPARING BIRDS

Pluck all birds unless they are scavengers or seabirds, which should be skinned. Leaving the skin on other kinds of birds will retain more of their nutrients when cooked. Cut the neck off close to the body. Cut open the chest and abdominal cavity, and remove the insides. Save the neck, liver, heart, and gizzard, which are all edible. Before eating the gizzard, split it open and remove the stones and partially digested food. Cook in any

Almost all birds are edible.

desired fashion. Cook scavenger birds a minimum of twenty minutes to kill parasites.

MAMMALS

Mammals are a great source of meat and should not be overlooked as a viable food source. Signs that indicate the presence of mammals include well-traveled trails, usually leading to feeding, watering, or bedding areas; fresh tracks and droppings; and fresh bedding signs, such as nests, burrows, or trampled-down field grass. In *open sea ice regions,* animals like seals, walruses, and foxes are sources of meat. In *tundra regions,* large game such as caribou, musk oxen, sheep, wolves, and bears can be found. All will be hard to procure without a firearm. It's advisable to approach rivers and streams with caution in the spring, since bears are often fishing for salmon during this time of year. Bears feed on berries during the fall, so approach these areas with caution also. The tundra also provides a fair amount of small game, such as lemmings, mice, ground squirrels, marmots, and foxes, which can be trapped or killed year-round. In *forested cold-climate regions,*

Small game is easier than large game to procure without a rifle.

large game such as moose, deer, caribou, and bears, as well as small game like hares, squirrels, porcupines, muskrats, and beavers can be found.

The odds of procuring a big-game animal without a rifle are small, and the risk of injury from trying to snare one is too high. If you are out of food and want to catch a mammal, for best results, attempt to snare small game. It shouldn't be too hard to find their trails, located in heavy cover or undergrowth, or running parallel to roads and open areas. A simple loop snare is the best method of procurement in cold climates, since triggers often freeze or lose their spring.

SIMPLE LOOP SNARE

An animal caught in this type of snare will either strangle itself or be held secure until your arrival. To construct a simple loop snare, use either snare wire or improvised line (discussed earlier) that's strong enough to hold the mammal you intend to catch. If using snare wire, start by making a fixed loop at one end. To do this, bend the wire 2 inches from the end, fold it back on itself, and twist or wrap the end of the wire and its body together, leaving a small loop. Twist the fixed loop at its midpoint until it forms a figure eight. Fold the top half of the figure eight down onto the lower half. Run the free end of the wire through the fixed loop. The size of the snare

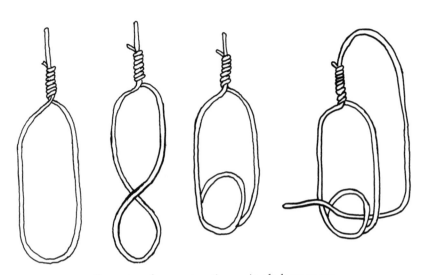

Four steps for constructing a simple loop snare

will determine the resultant circle's diameter. It should be slightly larger than the head size of the animal you intend to catch. In extremely cold weather, the lines can get brittle from the cold, so it's best to double the wire in order to prevent the snare from breaking.

If using improvised line, make a slipknot that tightens down when the animal puts its head through it and lunges forward.

Doubling the line will increase its strength.

Slipknot

Avoid removing the bark from any natural material used in the snare's construction. If the bark is removed, camouflage the exposed wood by rubbing dirt on it. Since animals avoid humans, it's important to remove your scent from the snare. One method of hiding your scent is to hold the snaring material over smoke or underwater for several minutes prior to its final placement. Place multiple simple loop snares, at least fifteen for every animal you want to catch, at den openings or well-traveled trails so that

Simple loop snare

Funneling helps move an animal into the snare.

the loop is at the same height as the animal's head. When placing a snare, avoid disturbing the area as much as possible. If establishing a snare on a well-traveled trail, try to use the natural funneling of any surrounding vegetation. If natural funneling isn't available, create your own. Attach the free end of the snare to a branch, rock, or drag stick (a big stick that either is too heavy for the animal to drag or will get stuck in the surrounding debris when the animal tries to move). Check your snares at dawn and dusk. Always make sure any caught game is dead before getting too close.

SQUIRREL POLE
A squirrel pole is an efficient means by which to catch multiple squirrels with a minimal amount of time, effort, or materials. Attach several simple loop snares to a pole approximately 6 feet long, then lean the pole onto an area with multiple squirrel feeding signs (look for mounds of pinecone

Squirrel pole

scales, usually on a stump or a fallen tree). The squirrel will inevitably use the pole to try to get to his favorite feeding site.

RODENT SKEWER

A forked spear made from a long sapling can be used as a rodent skewer. To use it, thrust the pointed end into an animal hole until you feel the animal. Twist the stick so that it gets tightly snagged in the animal's fur, then pull the animal out of the hole. The rodent will try to bite and scratch you if it can, so keep it at a distance. Use a club or rock to kill it.

Rodent skewer

PREPARING GAME

In order to eat your catch, you'll first need to skin, gut, and butcher most game. Always do this well away from your camp and your food cache. Before skinning an animal, be sure it is dead. Once you're sure, cut the animal's throat, and collect the blood in a container for later use. If time is not an issue, wait thirty minutes before starting to skin. This allows the body to cool, which makes it easier to skin and also gives enough time for most parasites to leave the animal's hide.

Glove skinning is most often used for skinning small game. Hang the animal from its hid legs and make a circular cut just above the leg joints. Don't cut through the tendon! To avoid dulling your knife by cutting from the fur side, slide a finger between the hide and muscle and place your knife next to the muscle so that you cut the hide from the inside. Cut down the inside of each leg, ending close to the genital area, and peel the skin off of the legs until you reach the animal's tail. Firmly slide a finger under the hide between the tail and spine until you have a space that allows you to cut the tail free. Do the same on the front side. At this point the hide can be pulled down and free from the animal's membrane with little effort. Avoid squeezing the belly since this may cause urine to spill onto the meat. Pull the front feet through the hide (inside out) by sliding a finger between the elbow and the membrane and pulling the leg up and free from the rest of the hide. Cut off the feet. The head can either be severed or skinned depending on your talents.

A larger animal can be hung from a tree by its hind legs or skinned while lying on the ground. To hang it by its hind legs, find the tendon that connects the upper and lower leg and poke a hole between it and the bone. If musk glands are present, remove them. (Musk glands are usually found at the bend between the upper and lower parts of the hind legs.) Free the hide from the animal's genitals by cutting a circular area around them, and then make an incision that runs just under its hide and all the way up to the neck. To avoid cutting the entrails, slide your index and middle finger between the hide and the thin membrane enclosing the entrails. Use the V between the fingers to guide the cut and push the entrails down and away from the knife. Next, cut around the joint of each extremity. From there, extend the cut down the insides of each leg until it reaches the midline incision. You should attempt to pull off the hide using the same method as for small game. If you need to use your knife, be sure to cut toward the meat so as to not damage the hide (avoid cutting through the entrails or the hide). If skinning on the ground, use the hide to protect the meat, and don't remove it until after you gut and butcher the animal. Once the hide has been removed it can be tanned and used for clothing, shelter, cover and containers.

To gut an animal, place the carcass, belly up, on a slope, or hang it from a tree by its hind legs. Make a small incision just in front of the anus, and insert your index and middle finger into the cut, spreading them apart to form a V. Slide the knife into the incision between the V formed by your two fingers. Use your fingers to push the internal organs down, away from the knife, and as a guide for the knife as you cut up the abdominal cavity to the breastbone. Avoid cutting the bladder or other internal organs. If the bladder or internal organs are punctured, wash the meat as soon as possible. Cut around the anus and sex organs so that they will be easily removed with the entrails.

Remove the intact bladder by pinching it off close to the opening and cutting it free. Remove the entrails, pulling them down and away from the carcass. To do this, you will need to sever the intestines at the anus. Save the liver and kidneys for later consumption. If the liver is spotted, this is a sign of disease; discard all internal organs and thoroughly cook the meat. Cut through the diaphragm, and reach inside the chest cavity until you can touch the windpipe. Cut or pull the windpipe free, and remove the chest cavity contents. Save the lungs and heart for later consumption. All internal organs can be cooked in any fashion but are best when used in a stew.

Small game, such as rabbits, can be dressed without a knife. To do this, firmly grasp the rabbit between both hands at its rib cage and squeeze toward the stomach. Using a firm grip, raise the rabbit over your head and then fling it down hard, allowing your arms to go between your legs. This will cause the entrails to be expelled. Singe the hair off in a fire.

If you intend to eat the liver, you'll need to remove the small black sac or gallbladder, as it's not edible. If it breaks, wash the liver immediately to avoid tainting the meat. Since fat spoils quickly, it should be cut away from the meat and promptly used. The fat is best in soups.

To butcher an animal, cut the legs, back, and breast sections free of

Dressing small game without a knife

one another. When butchering large game, cut it into meal-size roasts and steaks that can be stored for later use. Cut the rest of the meat along the grain into long, thin strips about ⅛ inch thick, to be preserved by smoking or sun drying. The head meat, tongue, eyes, and brain are all edible, as is the marrow inside bones. Keep the bones, sinew, hooves, and other parts. Each will serve many different survival needs.

COOKING METHODS

In addition to killing parasites and bacteria, cooking your food can make it more palatable. There are many different ways to prepare game, and some are better than others from a nutritional standpoint. Boiling is best, but only if you drink the broth, which contains many of the nutrients cooked out of the food. Fried food tastes great, but frying is probably the worst way to cook something, as a lot of nutrients are lost during the process.

BOILING

Boiling is the best cooking method. If a container is not available, it may be necessary to improvise one. You might use a rock with a bowl-shaped center, but avoid rocks with a high moisture content, as they may explode. A thick, hollowed-out piece of wood that can be suspended over the fire may also serve as a container. If your container cannot be suspended over the fire, stone boiling is another option. Use a hot bed of coals to heat up numerous stones. Get them really hot. Set your container of food and water close to your bed of hot stones, and add rocks to it until the water begins to boil. To keep the water boiling, cover the top with bark or another improvised lid, and keep it covered except when removing or adding stones. Don't expect a rolling, rapid boil with this process, but a slow, steady bubbling should occur.

FRYING

Place a flat rock on or next to the fire. Avoid rocks with a high moisture content, as they may explode. Let the rock get hot, and cook on it as you would with a frying pan.

BROILING

Broiling is ideal for cooking small game over hot coals. Before cooking the animal, sear its flesh with the flames from the fire. This will help keep the juices, containing vital nutrients, inside the animal. Next, run a non-poisonous skewer—a branch that is small, straight, and strong—along the underside of the animal's backbone. Suspend the animal over the coals.

STORING FOOD

KEEP IT ALIVE

If able, keep all animals alive until you're ready to consume them. This ensures that the meat stays fresh. If it's a small rodent or rabbit, it may attract big game, so you'll need to protect it from becoming a coyote's meal instead of yours. This doesn't apply, of course, if you are using the rodent for bait.

A tree cache will help protect your food from bears and rodents.

COLD STORAGE

In winter, freeze the meat in meal-size portions to avoid spoilage from constant thawing and freezing. Another winter option is to bury the food in a snow refrigerator. During nonwinter months, you can create a refrigerator by digging a 2-foot hole in a moist, shady location. Put your food in a waterproof container, surround it with vegetation, and place it inside the pit. Cover with sticks and dirt until the hole is filled.

SURVIVAL TIPS

IF YOU DON'T HAVE WATER, DON'T EAT

It takes water to process food, and without water to replace what is lost, you'll accelerate the dehydration process.

AVOID GRASS SEEDS THAT ARE PURPLE OR BLACK

These colors indicate a fungus contamination, which if eaten can cause severe illness or even death.

AVOID MUSHROOMS

Mushrooms have almost no nutritional value, and since so many are poisonous, the risk is not worth the benefit.

OVERCOME FOOD AVERSIONS

If you can't stomach eating a cooked insect, cut it into pieces and put it into a soup or stew.

10

Navigating

As long as you are able to meet your survival needs, stay put. Rescue attempts are far more successful when searching for a stationary survivor. However, there are three situations when you might need to consider traveling from your present location to another.

1. If your present location doesn't have adequate resources to meet your needs (e.g., personal protection, sustenance, signaling).
2. If rescue doesn't appear to be imminent.
3. If you know your location and have the navigational skills to travel to safety.

MAP AND COMPASS

A map and compass are the basic tools that most backcountry travelers use for navigating in the wilderness.

MAP NOMENCLATURE

The particulars of any map's nomenclature can usually be found within its main body and the surrounding margins. For a map to be an effective tool, you must become familiar with the one you're using before departing for the wilderness, as there are several different types of maps available. The basic components of most commercial maps are as follows:

Scale

A map's scale refers to the ratio of distances on the map to corresponding distances in real life. The following are commonly used scales:

1:24,000 scale: every inch on the map represents 24,000 inches in natural terrain.

1:64,000 scale: every inch on the map represents 64,000 inches in natural terrain.

Series

The series of a map refers to the amount of latitude and longitude displayed on the map. The following are commonly used series:

15-minute series: map covers 15 minutes of latitude and 15 minutes of longitude.

7.5-minute series: map covers 7.5 minutes of latitude and 7.5 minutes of longitude. (It would take four of these maps to cover the same surface area as one 15-minute series map.)

Colors and symbols

The color and symbols on a map denote different things and are very useful in evaluating the terrain. The most common colors and their meanings are as follows:

Green: woodland.

White: nonforested areas, such as rocks or meadows.

Blue: water.

Black: man-made structures, such as buildings or trails.

Red: prominent man-made items, such as major roads.

Brown: contour lines.

Contour lines

Contour lines are imaginary lines, superimposed on a topographic map, that connect points of equal elevation. The contour line interval, usually found in the map's margins, is the distance between two contour lines. The actual distance varies from one map to the next. The following is a basic guide on how to interpret the lay of the land as shown by a map's contour lines:

Lines close together: steep terrain.

Lines relatively far apart: gradual elevation gain or loss.

Lines form a V pointing toward a higher elevation: drainage.

Lines form a V pointing away from higher elevation: ridgeline.

Lines forming a circle: peak.

Magnetic variation

The magnetic variation is usually listed at the bottom of a topographic map. An arrow labeled "MN" indicates magnetic north; a second line, with a star at the end, is true north. Maps are set up for true north. This variation,

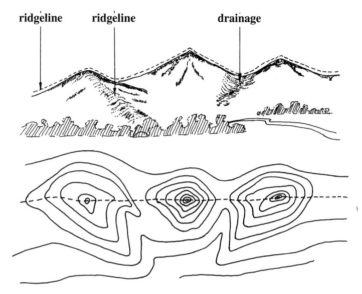

Contour lines are two-dimensional representations of the three-dimensional terrain.

Magnetic variation allows you to adjust the difference between true north and magnetic north.

commonly called declination, is valuable in compensating for the difference between true north and magnetic north, which will be your compass heading.

Latitude and longitude lines
Latitude and longitude lines are imaginary lines that encircle the globe, creating a crisscross grid system. These lines help you identify your location.

Latitude lines
These are east-west-running lines numbered from 0 to 90 degrees north and south of the equator. The 0-degree latitude line runs around the globe at the equator, and from there the numbers rise to north 90 degrees and south 90 degrees. In other words, the equator is 0 degrees latitude, the North Pole is 90 degrees north latitude, and the South Pole is 90 degrees south latitude. Latitude is often noted at the extreme ends of the horizontal map edges.

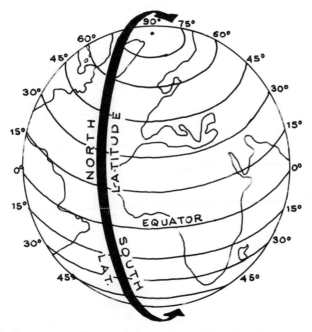

Latitude lines run east/west and are numbered from 0 to 90 degrees north and south of the equator.

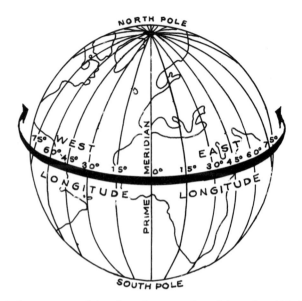

*Longitude lines run north/south and are numbered from 0 to 180 degrees
east and west of Greenwich England (the prime meridian).*

Longitude lines

These are north-south-running lines numbered from 0 to 180 degrees east
and west of Greenwich, England, the line commonly referred to as the prime
meridian. Longitude lines begin at 0 at Greenwich, England, traveling east
and west until they meet at the 180th meridian, which is often referred to as
the international dateline. The 0 meridian becomes the 180th meridian once
it intersects the extreme north and south sections of the globe. Longitude is
often noted at the extreme ends of the vertical map edges.

Rules for reading latitude and longitude

Both latitude and longitude lines are measured in degrees (°), minutes ('),
and seconds ("). There are 60 minutes between each degree and 60 seconds
between each minute. It's also important to distinguish north from south
when defining your latitude, and east from west for longitude. Whenever
giving latitude and longitude coordinates, always read the latitude first.

Latitude: A latitude might read, for example, 45° 30' 30". If north of the
equator, your latitude would be 45 degrees, 30 minutes, and 30 seconds

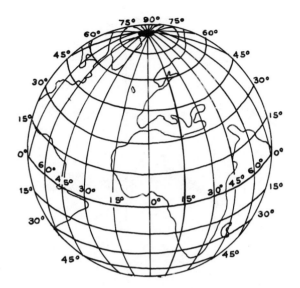

Whenever giving a latitude and longitude intersection, always read the latitude number first.

north latitude; if south of the equator, 45 degrees, 30 minutes, and 30 seconds south latitude. A latitude line will never be over 90 degrees north or south.

Longitude: A longitude might read, for example, 120° 30' 30". If east of the prime meridian, your longitude would be 120 degrees, 30 minutes, and 30 seconds east longitude; if west of the prime meridian, 120 degrees, 30 minutes, and 30 seconds west longitude. A longitude line will never be over 180 degrees east or west.

COMPASS NOMENCLATURE
This section describes an orienteering compass and compasses of similar structure, with a circular housing mounted on a rectangular base.

Rectangular base plate
The sides of the base plate have millimeter and inch markings, used to relate a map measurement to that of a relative field distance. The front has a direction-of-travel arrow. The arrow is parallel to the long edge and

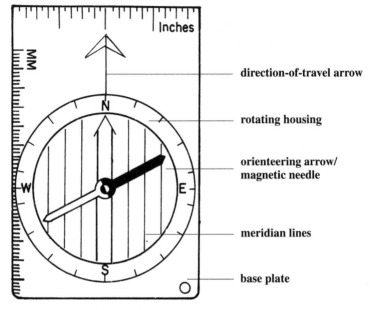

Orienteering compass nomenclature

perpendicular to the short edge. Compass headings are read from the point where the bottom of the direction-of-travel arrow touches the numbers on the edge of the circular compass housing. If the direction of travel arrow is not present or centered on the circular housing, your compass will probably have a stationary index line, sometimes called an index pointer. This nonmoving short white line is either located on the base plate next to the circular housing or inside the circular housing just beneath the moving numbers (it will be centered on the short wall of the base plate and on the same side of the compass as the direction of travel arrow). Headings are read where the numbers touch or pass over this line. The direction-of-travel arrow must always point toward the intended destination when a heading is being taken.

Circular housing

A rotating circular housing sits on the base plate. Its outer ring is marked with the four cardinal points (N, S, E, W) and degree lines starting at north and numbered clockwise to 360 degrees. The bottom of the housing has an etched orienting arrow, which points toward the north marking on the outer ring.

Magnetic needle

The compass needle sits beneath the circular housing. The needle is magnetic, and if you hold the compass too close to metal objects, the needle will be drawn toward them. It floats freely, and one end, usually red, points toward magnetic north (not true north). Magnetic north lies near Prince of Wales Island in northern Canada. Observe below how the magnetic variance affects readings done in the United States. Notice the line that passes through the Great Lakes and along the coast of Florida. This line is an agonic line, which has no variation. In other words, a compass heading of 0 or 360 degrees would point toward both magnetic and true north. The other lines, which are isogonic lines, have variations from true north. The line that extends through Oregon has a variation of 20 degrees east. When

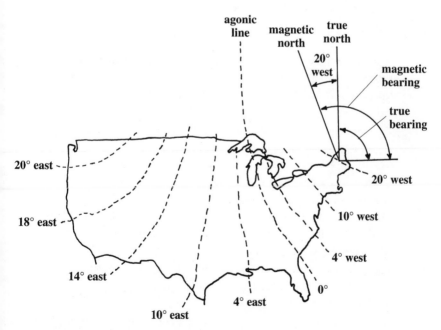

Agonic and Isogonic lines depict the variation between magnetic and true north.

this line is extended, the compass bearing of 360 is 20 degrees to the east of true north. The opposite would be true for the line extending through Maine. In this case, a compass bearing of 360 would be 20 degrees west of true north. Because of these variations, adjustments must be made in order to use a map and compass together.

USING YOUR MAP AND COMPASS TOGETHER
Anytime you're traveling in the wilderness, you should maintain a constant awareness of your general location. This awareness will help you pinpoint your location once you have completed the triangulating process (below).

Orienting Your Map
Orienting the map aligns its features to those of the surrounding terrain. This process is extremely helpful in determining your specific location.

1. Get to high ground. This will help you to evaluate the terrain once the map is oriented.
2. Open the map and place it on a flat, level surface. If possible, protect it from the dirt and moisture with something such as a poncho.
3. Rotate the circular housing on the compass, until the bottom of the direction-of-travel arrow is touching the true north heading. When doing this, you must account for the area's given declination. Declination is the difference between magnetic north (MN) and true north (★). True north is north as represented on a map, and magnetic north is the compass heading. In other words, a 360-degree map heading—true north— is not necessarily a 360-degree compass heading. This variation is usually depicted on the bottom of most topographic maps. If magnetic north is located west of true north, which is the case for most of the eastern United States, you would add your declination to 360 degrees. The resultant bearing would be the compass heading equivalent to true north at that location. If magnetic north is located east of true north, which is the case for most of the western United States, you would sub- tract your declination from 360 degrees. The resultant bearing would be the compass heading equivalent to true north at that location.
4. Set the compass on the map, with the edge of the long side resting next to, and parallel to, the left north-south margins (on USGS maps the map's left edge is a longitude line). Be sure that the direction-of- travel arrow is pointing toward the north end of the map.

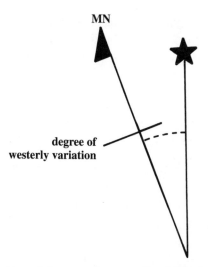

If magnetic north is west of true north, add the variation to 0 degrees.

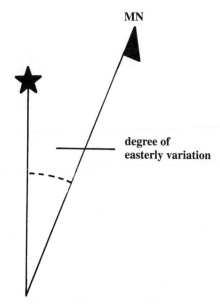

If magnetic north is east of true north, subtract the variation from 360 degrees.

5. Holding the compass in place on the map, rotate the map and compass until the floating magnetic needle is inside the etched orienting arrow of the base plate, with the red portion of the needle forward. This is called boxing the needle.
6. Double-check to ensure that the compass is still set for the variation adjustment, and if correct, weigh down the map edges to keep it in place.

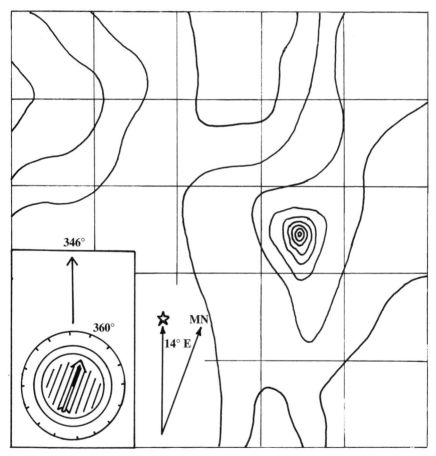

Be sure to account for the magnetic variation when orienting the map with a compass.

7. At this point, the map is oriented to the lay of the land, and the map features should reflect those of the surrounding terrain.

Triangulating to Determine Your Position

Triangulating is a process of identifying your specific location. For best results, get to high ground with 360 degrees of visibility.

1. Orient the map as outlined above.
2. Positively identify three of the surrounding landmarks, ideally 120 degrees apart, on your map by using the following guidelines:
   - Contour: Evaluate the landmark's contour, translating it into a two-dimensional appearance, and search for a matching contour outline on your map.
   - Distance: Determine the distance from your present position to the landmark to be identified. This may be estimated as follows:

     From 1 to 3 kilometers, you should be able to see the individual branches of a tree.

     From 3 to 5 kilometers, you should be able to see individual trees.

     From 5 to 8 kilometers, a group of trees will look like a green plush carpet.

     At greater than 8 kilometers, not only will the trees appear like a green plush carpet, but there will also be a bluish tint to the horizon.
   - Elevation: Determine your landmark's height as compared with that of your location.
3. Using your compass, point the direction-of-travel arrow at one of the identified landmarks, and then turn the compass housing until the etched orienting arrow boxes the magnetic needle (red end forward). At the point where the direction-of-travel arrow intersects the compass housing, read and record the magnetic bearing. Repeat this process for the other two landmarks.
4. Before working further with the map, ensure that it's still oriented.
5. Place the front left tip of the long edge of the compass on the identified map landmark, and while keeping the tip in place, rotate the compass until the magnetic needle is boxed (red end forward). Double-check that your compass heading is correct for the landmark being used.

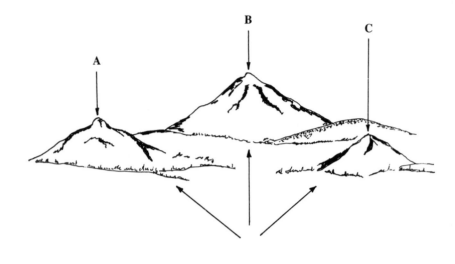

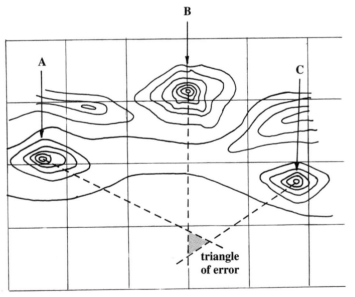

When triangulating, your position should be located somewhere within or around the triangle of error.

6. Lightly pencil a line from the landmark down, following the left edge of the compass base plate. You may need to extend the line. Repeat this process for the other two landmarks. Each time, double-check the map to ensure that it's still oriented.
7. Ultimately, a triangle will form where the three lines intersect. Your position should be located within or around the triangle.
8. For final position determination, evaluate the surrounding terrain and how it relates to the triangle displayed on the map.

ESTABLISHING A FIELD BEARING

Never travel unless you know both your present position and where you intend to go.

Establishing a field bearing with a map and compass:

1. Orient your map to the lay of the land.
2. Lightly draw a pencil line from your present location to your intended destination.
3. Place the top left edge of the compass on your intended destination.
4. Rotate the compass until the left edge is directly on and parallel to the line you drew.
5. Rotate the compass housing—keeping the base of the compass stationary—until the floating magnetic needle is boxed inside the orienting arrow (red portion of the needle forward).
6. Read the compass heading at the point where the bottom of the direction-of-travel arrow touches the numbers of the circular compass housing. This heading is the field bearing to your intended destination.

Establishing a field bearing with only a compass:

1. Holding the compass level, point the direction-of-travel arrow directly at your intended destination site.
2. Holding the compass in place, turn its housing until the magnetic needle is boxed directly over and inside the orienting arrow (red portion of the needle forward).
3. Read the heading at the point where the bottom of the direction-of-travel arrow touches the numbers of the circular housing. This heading is the field bearing to your intended destination.

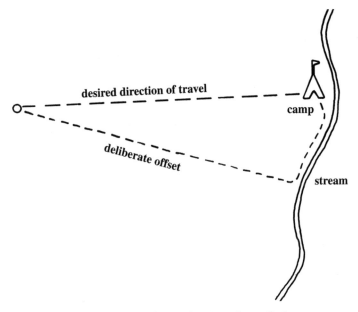

Using a deliberate offset makes it easier to find camp.

Deliberate offset

If your destination is a road or waterway, consider a heading with a deliberate offset, using a field heading several degrees to one side of your final location. Since it is very difficult to be precise in wilderness travel, this offset will help you in deciding whether to turn left or right once you intersect the road.

MAINTAINING A FIELD BEARING

Point-to-Point Navigation

Pick objects in line with your field bearing. Once one point is reached, recheck your bearing and pick another. This method allows you to steer clear of obstacles.

Following the Compass

Holding the compass level, and while keeping the magnetic needle boxed, walk forward in line with the direction-of-travel arrow.

start

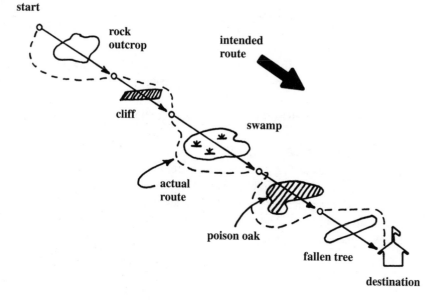

Point-to-point navigation allows you to steer clear of obstacles.

TRAVEL CHECKLIST

Before departing, write a travel checklist. The list will help you maintain your course and determine your exact location throughout your route.

1. Heading: Establish the compass heading, or azimuth, to your desired location. Once confident of your azimuth, trust your compass and stay on your heading.

2. Distance: Determine the total number of kilometers your route will cover.

3. Pace count: Estimate the number of paces it will take to reach your final destination (a pace is measured each time the same foot hits the ground). On fairly level terrain, it takes approximately 650 paces to go 1 kilometer. On steep terrain, the number of paces will nearly double for each kilometer.

4. Terrain evaluation: Evaluate your route's major terrain feature, such as a road or clearing, and determine how many paces it takes to each. By doing this, you'll maintain a constant awareness of your location within your route of travel.

5. Point description: Take the time to evaluate the appearance of your final location. This will help you when the time comes to evaluate whether you have had a successful trip.
6. Estimated arrival time: Estimating your arrival time will help you set realistic goals on the distance to travel each day.

DETERMINING DIRECTION WITHOUT A COMPASS

USING A STICK AND SHADOW
On a flat, level area, clear away all debris from a 3-foot circle until dirt is all that remains. Sharpen both ends of a long, straight stick, and then push one end into the ground until the stick's shadow falls onto the center of the cleared area. Mark the shadow tip with a twig or other appropriate material. Wait approximately ten minutes, and place another twig at the shadow

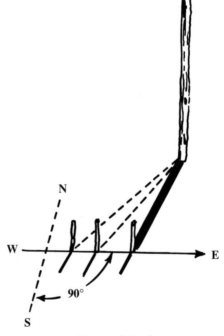

Stick and shadow

tip's new location. Draw a straight line between the two markers, and then another line perpendicular to it. Since the sun rises in the east and sets in the west, the first marking on the shadow line is west and the second one is east. The perpendicular line points to the north and south.

In the Northern Hemisphere, the sun will be south of your location, and in the Southern Hemisphere, the sun side will be north of you. This is not always true, however, and depending on where you are, the stick and shadow may not even be an option for use. The following guidelines will help you decide when to use a stick and shadow to determine your cardinal directions:

> For the stick and shadow method to be reliable, it cannot be used at greater than 66.6 degrees north or south latitude.
>
> Between 23.4 and 66.6 degrees north or south latitude, the sun's shadow will be north or south (respectively) of your location.
>
> Between 0 and 23.4 degrees north or south latitude, the sun can be north or south of your location, depending on the time of year. This poses no problem; simply realize that the first shadow is west, and the subsequent shadows move toward the east.

NIGHT VERSION OF THE STICK AND SHADOW

At night, most travelers use the North Star, called Polaris, or the Southern Cross, along with pointer stars, to determine the cardinal directions. If you cannot find these stars or constellations, you may opt to use stars or planets—located on the horizon away from the celestial poles—to determine the cardinal directions. Since these stars generally move from east to west, they can provide the same east-west line as made with the stick and shadow. Find a straight, 5-foot stick, and push it into the ground at a slight angle. Tie a piece of line to the top of the stick, ensuring that it is long enough to reach the ground with lots to spare. Lying on your back, position yourself so that you can pull the cord tautly, and hold it next to your temple. Move your body around until the taut line is pointing directly at the selected noncircumpolar star or planet. At this point, the line represents the star's shadow. Place a rock at the place where the line touches the ground, and repeat the process every ten minutes or so. As with the stick and shadow, the first mark is west and the second one is east. A perpendicular line will aid you in determining north and south.

Night stick and shadow

If you travel at night, use a sturdy, 7-foot-long walking stick. Keep the stick in front of you to protect your face from branches and to feel for irregularities on the ground.

NAVIGATING WITH A WATCH

Northern Hemisphere

Point the watch's hour hand toward the sun. Holding it in this position, draw an imaginary line midway between the hour hand and 12:00 (1:00 if daylight saving time). This imaginary line represents a southern heading. Draw another line perpendicular to this one to determine east and west.

Southern Hemisphere

In the Southern Hemisphere, point the watch's 12:00 symbol (1:00 if daylight saving time) toward the sun. Holding the watch in this position, draw an imaginary line midway between the 12:00 symbol and the hour hand. This imaginary line provides an approximate northern heading. Draw another line perpendicular to the original one to determine east and west.

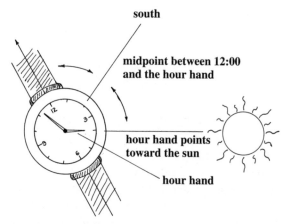

Proper technique for using a watch to determine a southern heading when north of the equator

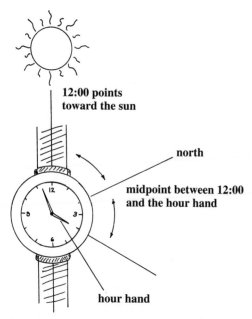

Proper technique for using a watch to determine a northern heading when south of the equator

CONSTELLATIONS

Northern Hemisphere

In the Northern Hemisphere, Cassiopeia and the Big Dipper are very useful tools for helping you find Polaris, the North Star. The Big Dipper looks like a cup with a long handle. Cassiopeia is made up of five stars that form a large W, with its opening facing the Big Dipper. During a twenty-four-hour period, the Big Dipper and Cassiopeia will do a complete rotation around Polaris. Halfway between these constellations, Polaris can be found. It is located at the very end of the Little Dipper's handle. Contrary to popular belief, it is not the brightest star in the sky, but instead is rather dull. It is always within 1 degree of true north at any given time of the year.

When both constellations cannot be seen, you can still find Polaris or determine your cardinal directions by doing one of the following:

- At the forward tip of the Big Dipper, there are two stars. Extend a line approximately four to five lengths beyond the second star to find Polaris.

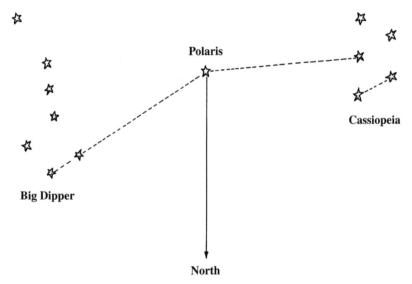

In the northern hemisphere, the Big Dipper and Cassiopeia can be utilized to find the northern cardinal direction.

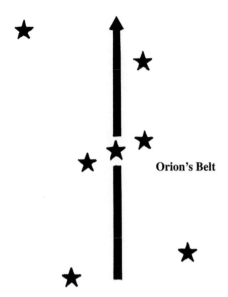

Orion rises in the east and sets in the west.

- From the center of Cassiopeia, extend a line out approximately four to five times the distance measured between any two of its stars to find Polaris.
- Orion the hunter circles the earth directly above the equator. The leading star of Orion's Belt (called Mintaka) rises exactly due east and sets exactly due west. The belt is formed by three close stars in line at the center of the figure. When Orion is not directly on the horizon, its east-west path makes it ideal for use with a night stick and shadow.

Southern Hemisphere

To find the cardinal directions in the Southern Hemisphere, use the Southern Cross, a constellation with four bright stars that look as though they are at the tips of a cross, and the Pointer Stars. The False Cross looks similar to the Southern Cross, and it may present a problem. The False Cross is less bright than the Southern Cross, and its stars are more widely spaced. In fact, the southern and eastern arms of the actual Southern Cross are two

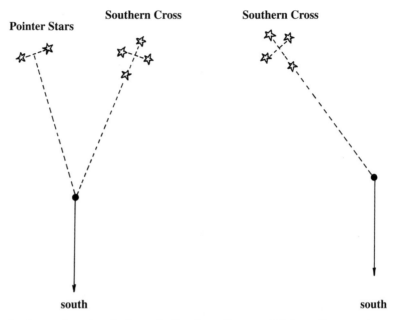

In the southern hemisphere, the Southern Cross and Pointer Stars can be utilized to find the southern cardinal direction.

of the brightest stars in the sky. The Pointer Stars are two stars that are side by side and in close proximity to the Southern Cross.

To establish a southern heading, extend an imaginary line from the top toward the bottom and out of the bottom of the cross. Draw another imaginary line perpendicular to the center of the Pointer Stars. At the point where the lines intersect, draw a third line straight down toward the ground. This line represents a southern direction.

GLOBAL POSITIONING SYSTEM (GPS)

A Global Positioning System (GPS) is a tool that can augment solid navigation skills but should *never* replace them. Learn how to use a map and compass before ever laying hands on a GPS! The GPS is an electronic device that works by capturing satellites' signals. To identify your location, given in latitude and longitude coordinates, it must lock on to three satellites; to identify your altitude, it must lock on to 4 satellites. As with all

Garmin GPS

electronic devices, a GPS is vulnerable to heat, cold, moisture, and sand. And even though satellites' signals are now easier than ever to capture, there are still times when a signal cannot be obtained. In such instances, the GPS is nothing more than added weight to the pack. It's a great tool, but don't rely on it for your sole source of navigation.

SURVIVAL TIPS

LEARNING TO NAVIGATE TAKES TIME
Practice is the key, and you should get lots of it. Knowing how to navigate may even allow you to rescue yourself by walking out.

NEVER GO INTO THE WILDERNESS WITHOUT A MAP AND COMPASS, ALONG WITH A GENERAL IDEA OF WHERE YOU'RE GOING AND WHERE YOU ARE
Before departing, always establish an emergency heading, to the nearest well-traveled road, that will remain constant no matter where you are.

NEVER LEAVE YOUR CAMP OR SHELTER WITHOUT A HEADING,
AND PACE COUNT BACK
Otherwise you may not be able to find it when trying to return.

WHEN ON A GROSS HEADING, YOU CAN USE YOUR SHADOW TO
MAINTAIN A GENERAL DIRECTION OF TRAVEL
To do this, orient your shadow to the heading you're taking and keep it
there while hiking. Since the sun moves approximately 15 degrees an hour
you'll need to adjust your shadow's position, related to your heading, every
15 minutes or so.

11

Traveling on Snow and Ice

HOW TO LOAD YOUR PACK

When carrying an internal frame pack on a trail, organize your gear so that the heavier items are on top and close to your back. This method places most of the pack's weight on your hips, making it easier to carry. If you'll be traveling off-trail, organize the pack so that the heavy items are close to the back, from the pack's top to its bottom. With this method, most of the pack's weight is carried by your shoulders and your back, allowing you better balance.

BASIC TRAVEL TECHNIQUES

BREAKING TRAIL AND SETTING THE PACE

The person breaking trail is working harder than anyone else, and this job needs to be switched at regular intervals between the members of a team. If in a team, set your pace distance so that it is comfortable for all members. Remember the COLDER acronym (see chapter 4). If you have dropped layers of clothing and are still sweating, you're going too fast.

KICK-STEPPING

When traveling in snow, kick-stepping will not only make your ascent easier, but it will also make it easier for those who are following you. Using the weight of your leg, swing the toe of your boot into the snow, creating a step that supports at least the ball of your foot if going straight up, or at least half of your foot if traversing. If you're in a group and are leading an ascent using this technique, consider the strides of those who are following you.

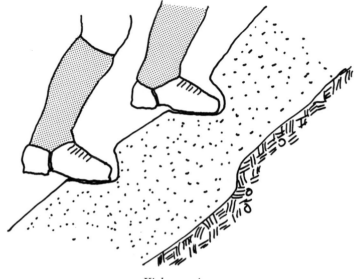

Kick-stepping

Plunge-stepping

When going uphill, lean forward until your body is perpendicular to the earth's natural surface—not that of the hill.

PLUNGE-STEPPING (DOWN-CLIMBING)
Plunge-stepping is similar to kick-stepping, except that you are going downhill and kicking your heels into the slope rather than your toes. Slightly bend the knees, and lean backward until your body is perpendicular to the ground at the base of the hill—not the hill's slope.

TRAVERSING
Traversing, or diagonal climbing, is a quick and easy method for getting up or down a hill. When traversing a hill, it may be necessary to slightly shorten your strides as the grade changes. It's times like this that an adjustable pole would be nice. This same technique can be used to descend a hill.

Traversing uphill

USING A RIDGELINE TO YOUR ADVANTAGE
When traveling in mountainous terrain, try to stay high on the ridgeline as much as you can. It is better to travel a little farther than to deal with the constant up-and-down travel associated with frequent elevation changes.

REST STEP
When walking uphill, use a rest step, which is done by locking the knee with each step. This process takes the weight off the muscle, allowing it to rest, and places it on the skeletal system. For best results, you'll need to take a short pause with each step.

TERRAIN ISSUES

CORNICES
Cornices are usually formed on the downwind, or leeward, side of a ridge. This happens as a result of the wind blowing snow off and over the windward side of a cliff, depositing it on the downwind side. If you are approaching a peak from the windward side, you may not be aware that a cornice

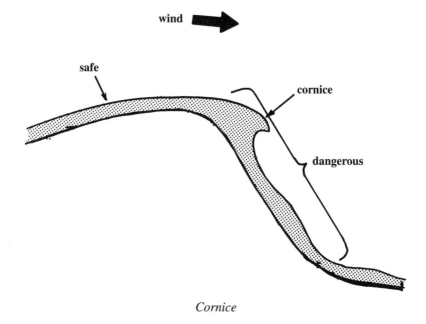

Cornice

exists. Since wind patterns are similar throughout an area, take the time to look at the downwind side of other peaks in your location. Try to identify a cornice in advance, and stay well below its potential fracture line. If you're unsure whether a cornice exists, keep your elevation well below the peak, going no higher than two-thirds of the way up the ridge. If approaching from the leeward side, look for wavelike formations that extend from the peak, and avoid these areas.

GLACIERS AND CREVASSES

A glacier is basically a snow and ice river that forms over many years. It is created when snow is in a location that doesn't allow it to melt before the next year's snowfall. Each year, new layers are added to the top of the glacier, and it loses some of its lower portion as it melts away. The point at which it melts occurs where the glacier is low enough that no new snow can accumulate and the temperatures are high enough to cause melting. Crevasses are cracks in a glacier that result when a glacier stretches or bends too fast. They often run about 100 feet deep. On occasion, low-elevation glaciers will completely fracture at a crevasse, causing an ice avalanche, which can be deadly. These usually occur during late summer and early fall. Unless you have achieved specific training in glacier travel, you should avoid these areas. If no other travel option exists, cross close to the top, where the glacier is more stable.

CREEKS

Crossing a creek is often a problem during the winter. If it's a small creek, loosen your pack's shoulder straps, and undo your waistband so you can quickly remove the pack if you fall in. Try to cross at a shaded area where there is a large amount of snow and no water can be seen. Take off your skis or snowshoes, and use a pole to evaluate the snow's depth and stability before taking each step. Cross one person at a time. For larger creeks where no bridge or road crossing is available, try to find a narrow area where passage is possible (you may need to travel upstream closer to the creek's origin to find such a place).

FROZEN BODIES OF WATER

Avoid crossing large bodies of ice—the risk associated with breaking through is too high. Always go around a lake. If approaching a river and you have no other choice but to cross, however, cross on the outside of a bend or at a straight stretch where the water is apt to be shallow. Avoid areas that have anything sticking up out of the ice, such as a log, stump, or rock, since radiant heat from the object will have weakened the ice directly next to it.

TREES AND ROCKS
In snowy conditions, trees and rocks can present problems for the back-country traveler. Steep-sided wells form around rocks and tree trunks, due to wind and the radiant heat that these objects produce. To avoid falling into these deep air pockets, avoid walking too close to exposed trees and rocks. Also, tree branches hoard snow, which gladly drops down the back of your neck when you pass by. When you have to pass under a tree, either shake the branches first or walk behind someone else.

USING AN ICE AX
When traveling in mountainous regions where snow or ice is present, always take along an ice ax. When not in use, the ice ax should be snugly secured on your pack or carried in one hand—at the balance point—so that it is parallel to the ground, with the pick toward the ground and the spike facing forward. The ice ax should have a long lanyard, the length of your reach plus 6 inches, attached to your wrist.

USING AN ICE AX TO SELF-BELAY
When self-belaying with an ice ax, the ax is used as an anchor that supports and stops your descent down the hill should you fall. When using the ice ax as a self-belay device, hold it so that the palm is on top of the adze and the thumb and index finger hang—on opposite sides—over the pick. A self-belay hold is employed when the ice ax is used for an anchor and to help with balance.

While Going Diagonally up a Slope
When going diagonally up a hill, hold the ax perpendicular to the slope's angle, one hand grasping the head while the other holds the shaft, which is jammed into the snow on the uphill side. Since the ice ax will cross in front of you, make sure the pick doesn't point toward your body. While the

Using an ice ax to go diagonally uphill

ax is planted in the snow, take one step with each foot, secure and balance yourself, and then pull the ax free. Move it forward on the uphill side, and replant it into the snow.

While Going Directly up a Slope
When going straight up a hill, always keep the ax on your uphill side, jam its spike deep into the snow's surface, and take one step with each foot, using a kick step. Once you are secure in your new position, pull the ice ax free and move it uphill, replanting it deep into the snow's surface, and repeat your two steps. Continue doing this until a belay is no longer needed.

Using an ice ax to go directly uphill

Using an ice ax to go downhill

While Going Down a Slope

When going straight down a hill, hold the ice ax in one hand on the downhill side with its spike pointing toward the snow's surface, and use a plunge step. This method keeps the ax ready to be jammed into the snow should you lose your balance. On steep slopes, the ax should be planted firmly into the snow on the downhill side every two steps (one with each foot) and used to help with balance and protection. On a very steep slope, you should face into the slope and, using a kick step, climb down the hill backward. When using this technique, the ax should be kept on the uphill side and continually planted and replanted after every two steps.

USING AN ICE AX TO SELF-ARREST

A self-arrest is used when you fall or your self-belay has failed. It will need to be implemented quickly once you have fallen and begun a rapid, out-of-control descent. If you're lucky, you'll fall on your belly with your head uphill and your feet facing downhill; if you're not lucky, you'll have to dig the ax pick in and turn and rotate your body until into this position. Regardless of your body's position, your goal is to stop yourself by using

Self-arrest

your weight, extremities, and ice ax. When using the ice ax as a self-arrest device, hold it so that your palm sits on the pick, your fingers draped over it on one side, and your thumb going under the adze next to the shaft. If you're using a self-belay grasp, when you fall, you'll need to switch to the self-arrest grasp quickly. For proper ax control, the ax should be held using the self-arrest grasp with one hand, grabbing as close to the point as you can with the other hand. Once you fall, the pick should be forced into the snow so that the adze is located between your ear and shoulder while perpendicular to your body's plane. The shaft should lie on a diagonal plane to your body, with the end opposite the adze and pick close to your hip. Press your chest down hard on the shaft of the ice ax. Your body weight will have a greater impact on forcing the pick into the snow than you can create using your arms. Keep your head down, and slightly arch your lower back away from the snow. These two maneuvers will increase the downward chest force upon the ax shaft. Spread your legs apart, and dig your knees and toes into the snow's surface.

USING AN ICE AX TO GLISSADE

A sitting glissade can be used to hasten your descent from a hill that poses no avalanche hazard. First remove your crampons so they don't get stuck in the snow and cause you to flip out of control. While wearing appropriate

Sitting Glissade

protective clothing, sit in the snow and begin sliding down the hill. Sit erect, with your knees bent and your feet flat on the surface. Hold the ice ax in the self-arrest position, with its tip scraping the snow on one side of your body.

TRAVELING ON SNOWSHOES

In general, it won't take long to learn the art of snowshoeing. Once they are strapped on, just start walking. When on a slope, you should carry an ice ax, on the uphill side, and use it as an anchor and support. An ice ax used for snowshoeing should extend 2 to 4 inches beyond the ground. This measurement is determined by standing erect while holding the ice ax in one hand (with fingers extended down its shaft) and pointing it straight down toward the ground. An ice ax can be used to help steady you while climbing by providing a third point of contact.

KICK-STEPPING

Kick-stepping on an ascent can be done with the Western, Bearpaw, and Beavertail style snowshoes. Use an ice ax as a self-belay to help anchor and balance your movement. To do this, keep it on the uphill side and plant its spike in the snow every two steps.

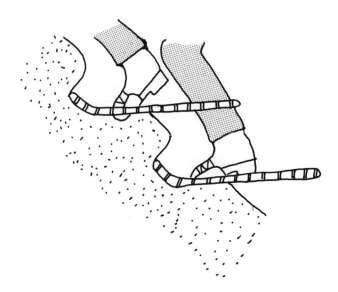

Kick-stepping uphill in snowshoes

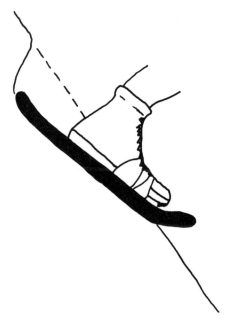

Walking downhill in snowshoes

DOWNHILL TRAVEL

When going down a gradual grade, slightly bend your knees, lean back, and point your toes down so that the snowshoes' crampons make full contact with the snow's surface. If the hill is too steep for this technique, either traverse down it or take off your snowshoes and descend by plunge-stepping.

TRAVERSING

To traverse with snowshoes, create a platform in the side of the hill by edging in, forcing the uphill side of the snowshoe into the slope, at least half of your foot width. As always, if in a group, consider the strides of those following you. It's times like this that an adjustable pole would be nice. This same technique can be used to come down a hill. All shoe types can be used for this technique. Use an ice ax as a self-belay to help anchor and balance your movement. To do this, keep it on the uphill side and plant its spike in the snow every two steps.

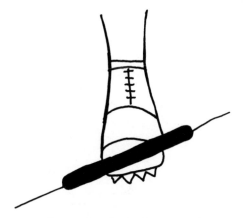

Traversing downhill in snowshoes

TRAVELING ON CROSS-COUNTRY SKIS

LEVEL TERRAIN

When traveling on level ground, the diagonal stride and double pole techniques are the most often used methods of cross-country skiing.

Diagonal Stride

The diagonal stride motion is similar to walking. Its rhythmic movement alternates from one leg (ski) to the other, while swinging a stabilizing opposite arm. Unlike walking, where the feet are picked up, you slide your feet over the surface, allowing a short pause at the end of each step so that the skis can glide across the snow. When the front ski ends its forward glide, you begin a kick by applying a downward tromping into the snow. Once the downward force begins, you bend your leg slightly, and then straighten it while pushing off and back, kicking the leg backward. A weight transfer to the kicking ski, in conjunction with continued downward force, is needed for best results. The opposite ski, having limited weight, will now easily glide forward. Repeating this process with first one foot and then the other will quickly move you to your destination. Tip slightly forward at the ankles, and keep your head up so that you can see what's coming. Your poles should move forward and backward in unison with the opposing feet: right pole

Diagonal stride

with left foot and vice versa. To hold the poles, insert your hands from the straps' underside. Lightly grip the handles; your pressure should focus primarily on the straps. To use a pole, plant it behind the heel, and allow it to move backward as you perform your kick and glide. Once it's behind the hip, relax your grip so that the pole maintains constant contact with the snow. Gently bring the pole forward as you start the backward motion on the opposite side.

Double-Pole

If the terrain or snow conditions are such that a diagonal stride is too slow or difficult to perform, using the double-pole technique is a good option. While keeping your legs relaxed and fairly straight, plant both poles in front of you, and use them to propel you forward. For maximum glide, no kick is initiated, and both skis are kept in full contact with the snow.

GOING UPHILL

Uphill techniques include taking off the skis and kick-stepping up; using a traverse, forward sidestep, or herringbone technique; or wearing skins.

Uphill Traverse

The uphill traverse, or diagonal climbing, is the easiest method for getting up a hill. As with the diagonal stride, continue a regular rhythm, but slightly

Double pole

Traversing uphill in cross-country skis

shorten your strides as the grade increases. It's at times like this that an adjustable pole would be nice. This same technique can be used to go down a hill.

Forward Sidestep

When space is limited or the snow is fairly firm, the forward sidestep method is ideal for getting up a hill in a hurry. To perform, simply lift and swing the uphill ski forward (with a slight diagonal path) and upslope in the direction of your travel. Follow with the downhill ski, using the same maneuver. You can also do a simple uphill sidestep, maneuvering the skis sideways up the hill. To prevent yourself from slipping downhill, make a slight cut into the snow with the uphill ski edge. This same technique can be used to go down a hill.

Cross-country ski forward sidestep

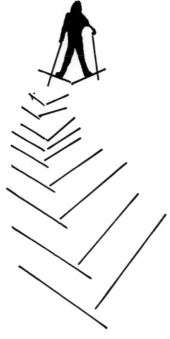

Herringbone

Herringbone

Although the herringbone method allows you to go straight up a slight hill, it probably isn't well suited for a steeper slope. Place your skis into a V position, angling only as much as needed. Then firmly planting the edges into the snow, walk up the hill, totally transferring your weight from one ski to the other.

Skins

Skins are long strips of nylon or similar material that adhere to the bottom of your skis, providing traction. The ideal size will cover the bottom of the ski but not its edges. The working side of the skin has a one-way nap that allows it to slide in one direction and catch in another. Skins are helpful on steep ascents or descents, where more traction is required.

GOING DOWNHILL

When going downhill, you can traverse, forward sidestep, or use skins. If you'd like a quicker descent, you may want to use a step turn, gliding wedge, or perhaps even telemark. Regardless of which method you use, when going downhill it is best to keep your knees slightly bent (enough to feel a bend in your ankles) and your hands out in front of you with poles angled behind.

Step Turn

The step turn is ideal for slight downhill slopes, as well as flat areas. To do a step turn to the right, move the right ski tip out and away from the body while keeping its tail in place. Finish by moving the left ski tip next to the right one.

Step turn

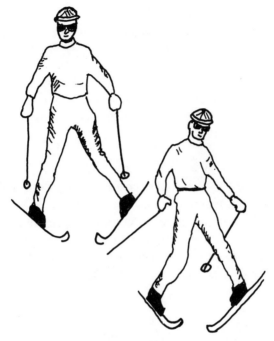

Gliding wedge

Gliding Wedge

The gliding wedge is similar to the snowplow technique used by downhill skiers. While in a wide stance with knees bent, make an A-shaped wedge, with your ski tips together, and dig the inside edges into the snow. The more pressure on the inner edges, the slower you will go. To turn, move your hips, knees, and feet toward the direction you want to go, while shifting your weight to the downhill ski.

Telemarking

Telemarking is an advanced skill primarily used in the mountains, allowing an individual to get to the bottom very fast. Its basic technique revolves around weight transfer and ski movement that allow you to turn while traversing down a hill. This skill is best learned on the slopes with a skilled instructor.

Skiing

If you have experience in cross-country skis or bindings that can secure the heel of your boot in place, you can actually ski down the hill.

GETTING UP AND TURNING

No matter where you go, sooner or later you will fall or need to turn. Getting up or making a turn while wearing cross-country skis may not be an easy task.

Getting Up

When, not if, you fall, it may take some effort to get back on your skis. You'll first need to squirm, kick, and roll until you can get your skis under your knees, with your toes pointing forward. The hardest part is getting into that position. Next, raise one knee, grasp your poles firmly, and place the poles perpendicular to the ground. While pushing down on the poles and with the thigh of the raised knee, move into the standing position.

Kick turn

Kick Turn

The kick turn allows you to change your direction 180 degrees. Planting your poles out wide and behind you will provide you the stability needed to perform this maneuver. Raise one ski up, and plant the back end into the snow so that the ski is about perpendicular to the ground. Pivot the ski out, and bring it back to the ground in its previous location, but pointing in the opposite direction. Pick up the other ski and swing it around and next to the first ski, so that they are side by side and facing in the same direction.

TRAVELING ON CRAMPONS

Traveling on ice or hard snow requires crampons, cleats that provide the needed traction for you to maintain contact with the surface instead of falling and going for a ride. If you are traveling in an area where the snow is hard enough to require crampons, make sure you have an ice ax, too.

SURVIVAL TIPS

TRAVELING IN SURVIVAL SITUATIONS

If you're in a survival situation where rescue doesn't appear imminent, the area you're in doesn't meet your needs, and you have solid navigational skills, you may elect to travel out to safety. If you do, leave a note for potential rescuers listing your time of departure, route, and intended destination. In addition, mark your trail by tying flags to branches and/or breaking branches.

REPAIRING A BROKEN SNOWSHOE

Most snowshoe breaks occur when the shoe is bridged between the ground and a log or similar object. When this happens, the pressure at the middle of the frame is too great, and the shoe breaks. Once the shoe has broken, it will be difficult to travel on until it's repaired. The best quick and simple fix is to tie a sturdy branch to the broken section so that it extends 3 to 4 inches beyond the break on both sides.

WHITEOUTS

A whiteout makes travel extremely difficult and dangerous. If one occurs, play it safe by building a shelter and staying put until the conditions clear.

12

Avalanches

Statistics have shown that 90 percent of all avalanche victims rescued within five minutes survive, but less than 50 percent are still alive after thirty minutes. These statistics, however, are proving to be far more favorable for individuals who use the AvaLung breathing device. Proper preparation and avalanche rescue knowhow are key to survival, since time is of the utmost importance. Educate yourself through reading and taking avalanche training classes. Learn about conditions, both past and present, where you intend to go: any hazards located in the area, such as slide paths, cornices, or crevasses, and the current weather report and avalanche dangers associated with it. Make sure all members of the group have compatible beacons. Most accidents could have been avoided through proper preparation. Take the time to do it, and if conditions seem questionable, go another day.

AVALANCHE TYPES

POINT RELEASE AVALANCHE
This type of avalanche begins at a single point and collects snow as it heads downhill, growing bigger and bigger. A point release avalanche occurs most often in the spring, when new snow falls on a smooth snow surface that was created by repeated thawing, freezing, or rain. The risk is high after heavy snowfall (10 to 12 inches total, or when it has fallen at more than 1 inch per hour).

SLAB AVALANCHES
A slab avalanche is a solid, cohesive layer of snow that slides all at once after breaking free from its bond to an underlying surface. Most avalanche

Point release avalanche

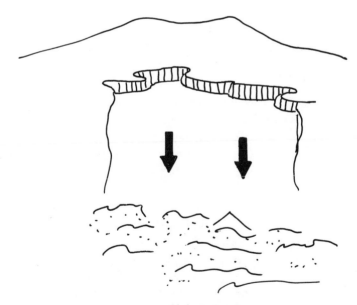

Slab avalanche

victims are caught in this type of avalanche. These usually occur during or after a winter storm and are often triggered by someone.

AVALANCHE TRIGGERS

Avalanches are usually triggered by humans or conditions related to recent weather changes. Most wilderness areas stay abreast of avalanche conditions and closely monitor the snow's condition for the potential of slides. In order to pass this information onto the backcountry traveler, the United States Avalanche Danger Descriptors guide was created. This guide provides a color reference to describe current avalanche conditions. This information should be used in addition to your judgment, experience, and knowledge of the area.

IDENTIFYING AVALANCHE HAZARDS

Four factors should be considered when evaluating the potential risk of an avalanche: terrain, snowpack, weather, and the human factor.

TERRAIN

A terrain's potential for an avalanche is based on the angle, aspect, and configuration of the slope.

Slope angle

A slope angle between 25 and 60 degrees has the potential to be an avalanche hazard. Most avalanches occur between 30 and 45 degrees. Steeper slopes rarely hold on to snow, and shallow slopes rarely produce enough momentum for the snow to slide. Unless you are highly experienced at measuring these angles, use a clinometer (see chapter 3).

Slope aspect

A slope's aspect describes its position in relation to the sun and wind. In winter, your odds are better when using slopes that have sun exposure, since the snow will normally settle and stabilize faster. In spring and summer, however, the sun-exposed slopes tend to be less stable, and odds favor slopes that had limited sun during the winter. Slopes that directly face the wind tend to be safer than those that don't, since the wind either rids them of new snow or packs it down. Leeward slopes, those sheltered from the

UNITED STATES AVALANCHE DANGER DESCRIPTORS

Danger Level (& Color)	Avalanche Probability and Avalanche Trigger	Degree and Distribution of Avalanche Danger	Recommended Action in the Backcountry
What	*Why*	*Where*	*What To Do*
LOW (green)	Natural avalanches very unlikely. Human triggered avalanches unlikely.	Generally stable snow. Isolated areas of instability.	Travel is generally safe. Normal caution is advised.
MODERATE (yellow)	Natural avalanches unlikely. Human triggered avalanches possible.	Unstable slabs possible on steep terrain.	Use caution in steeper terrain on certain aspects (defined in accompanying statement).
CONSIDERABLE (orange)	Natural avalanches possible. Human triggered avalanches probable.	Unstable slabs probable on steep terrain.	Be increasingly cautious in steeper terrain.
HIGH (red)	Natural and human triggered avalanches likely.	Unstable slabs likely on a variety of aspects and slope angles.	Travel in avalanche terrain is not recommended. Safest travel on windward ridges of lower angle slopes without steeper terrain above.
EXTREME (black)	Widespread natural or human triggered avalanches certain.	Extremely unstable slabs certain on most aspects and slope angles. Large, destructive avalanches possible.	Travel in avalanche terrain should be avoided and travel confined to low angle terrain well away from avalanche path run-outs.

AVALANCHE SAFETY BASICS

Avalanches don't happen by accident, and most human involvement is a matter of choice, not chance. Most avalanche accidents are caused by slab avalanches which are triggered by the victim or a member of the victim's party. However, any avalanche may cause injury or death and even small slides may be dangerous. Hence, always practice safe route finding skills, be aware of changing conditions, and carry avalanche rescue gear. Learn and apply avalanche terrain analysis and snow stability evaluation techniques to help minimize your risk. Remember that avalanche danger rating levels are only general guidelines. Distinctions between geographic areas, elevations, slope aspects, and slope angles are approximate and transition zones between dangers exist. No matter what the current avalanche danger there are avalanche-safe areas in the mountains.

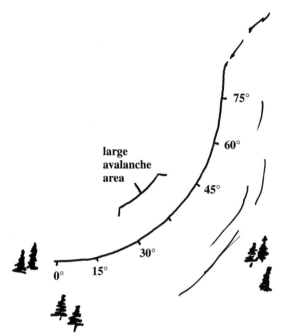

Slope angle

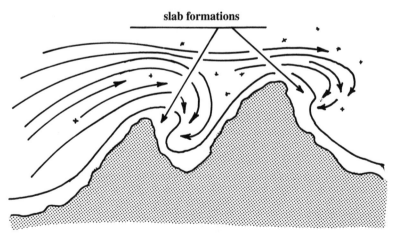

Slope aspect

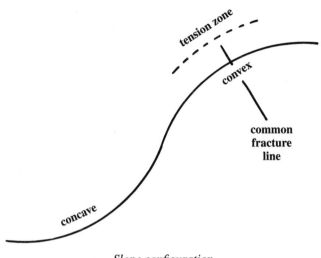

Slope configuration

wind, collect the snow blown off the windward side, resulting in cornices, deep unconsolidated snow, and wind slabs.

Slope configuration

Does the slope have a convex or concave appearance? Snow on a convex slope is under a great deal of tension and is more prone to release than snow covering a concave slope. A straight, open, and steep slope is an obvious hazard. Trees that are bent down and away from the upward slope and are missing limbs on the uphill side are signs that a major avalanche has traveled through that area.

SNOWPACK

A snowpack is created by episodes of intermittent storms, changes in weather, and temperature fluctuations. Through this process, multiple layers of consolidated snow are formed, one on top of the other. New layers may or may not adhere to the underlying layer. Slabs are formed when an upper cohesive layer does not bond with a thin, weak layer that sits underneath it. The stability of a snowpack can be evaluated by doing the Rutschblock test and paying close attention to Mother Nature's clues. However, it's important to consider all factors related to potential avalanche hazards.

Rutschblock Test
The Rutschblock test can be used to evaluate the stability of a slope and its potential to slide. In this test, the skier or snowshoer actually stands on a large block of snow to see if it can support his or her weight. The test should be performed on a slope that has similar conditions to the one you intend to approach. Using a shovel or snow saw (improvise if neither is available), cut three sides of a square block—the front and two sides—each about 6 feet long and 3 feet deep, or until the lower weaker layer is exposed. Using a saw, ski, or other improvised device, cut the back wall free of the

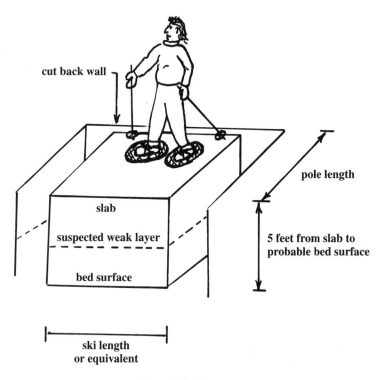

Rutschblock test

slope and to the same depth as the other sides. Wearing your skis or snow-shoes, step onto the center of the block, from the uphill side. Does the block support your weight? If it does, then safely do a series of jumps to see if the block slides free of the weaker surface. A slope is considered *extremely unstable* if the test slab breaks free while you are approaching the site, creating it, or simply standing on the block; a slope is considered *unstable* if the slab breaks free when you're flexing in preparation for the first jump or during the first jump itself; a slope is considered *relatively stable* when it takes repeated hard jumps to break the slab free; and a slope is considered *stable* when the slab doesn't fail after repeated jumps. Other tests may be used to evaluate a slope's stability, but they are not as reliable as the Rutschblock test, and it's difficult to interpret the value of the information they provide. If you are concerned about a slope's stability, take the time to do the Rutschblock test.

Nature's clues

Mother Nature provides clues about the snowpack's stability. Paying close attention to them will provide additional information about the relative risk associated with your present location.

Recent avalanches on similar slopes

This is probably the best clue you'll ever get, and it's advisable to avoid similar slopes.

Shooting cracks

A shooting crack could be a precursor to a slab avalanche. If snow conditions create this effect, avoid avalanche terrain.

Whumping noises

When a snowpack's weak layer collapses, it makes a *whump* sound. If you hear this sound, avoid avalanche terrain.

Hollow sounds

A hollow, drumlike sound radiating up from the snowpack may indicate that a weak layer is underneath an upper cohesive layer (slab) of snow. If you hear this sound, avoid avalanche terrain.

WEATHER

Snowfall, rain, wind, and temperatures all affect the bond between layers of snow.

Recent snowfall or rain

The risk of avalanche is extremely high after a heavy snowfall (10 to 12 inches total, or when it has fallen at more than 1 inch per hour). Rain penetrates the snow and weakens the bond between layers, making it easier for a slab to break free.

Wind

Wind-loaded snow forms slabs on the leeward side of a hill, making it a potential avalanche hazard. Avoid areas where wind loading is a concern. (Also see Slope Aspect, above.)

Temperatures

Warm or cool temperatures can create various conditions that may cause a greater potential for avalanche.

Warm temperatures

If warm temperatures do not occur rapidly, they will increase the density and bond of the snowpack, making it less prone to avalanche. A rapid warming trend, on the other hand, will weaken the snow, making the bond between layers less stable and more prone to human-triggered slab avalanches.

Depth hoar

Depth hoar is a layer of snow, close to the ground's surface, created when there is a significant difference in temperature between the snow's surface and the ground. It is composed of highly faceted snow crystals and cannot support much weight, making it a dangerous underlying layer that rarely bonds to the subsequent layers of snow that cover it. The risk of depth hoar formation is highest during the early season. If present, the potential for an avalanche is extremely high.

Surface hoar

Surface hoar is similar to dew and is created on the snow's surface when cool, cloudless, and calm nights are present. Like depth hoar, it doesn't bond well with subsequent snow cover, and its weak layer creates a potential avalanche hazard.

THE HUMAN FACTOR

All too often, individuals believe that no disaster will ever happen to them. They don't realize how often people have perished when decisions were based on similar attitudes. Travel decisions should be made on a multitude of factors, including everything discussed to this point. The group's attitude about the conditions, their goals, and the risks involved should all be considered, along with each member's technical skills, physical strength, and available equipment. Take the time to think things through. After all, traveling into the backcountry is supposed to be time spent having fun, not fighting for your life.

ROUTE SELECTION

Sometimes it may be necessary to cross an area that presents an avalanche risk. If this should be the case, try to avoid large, steep, leeward bowls, gullies, and cornices. Choose safer routes, such as ridgetops, valley floors, dense timber, and low-angle slopes. Before starting, remove ski pole straps; undo pack buckles for quick doffing; secure all zippers and openings on your clothing and gear; make sure your avalanche beacon is on and in the transmit mode; identify any safe islands that might be located in your route of travel, such as rocks or trees; and establish an escape route. Once ready, cross one person at a time, with all other members of the group watching. Try to cross at either the top or bottom of the slope; avoid the center, where escape may be impossible.

AVALANCHE NECESSITIES

AVALANCHE TRANSCEIVERS

All members in your group should carry avalanche transceivers (described in chapter 3) with fresh batteries. Before departing the trailhead, check your beacons by doing a walk-by. This is done by having one member's beacon turned to receive and having each other member walk by with his or her beacon on in the transmit mode. The receiving beacon should have an increased sound and visual signal as each member approaches. Don't forget to check the receiving beacon also. Once you've assured that all transceivers are working properly, turn them all to the transmit mode. If someone becomes buried, all other members of the party then switch to the receive mode to locate the victim.

OTHER AVALANCHE GEAR

Each member traveling into avalanche country should also carry a probe, a snow shovel, and an AvaLung (described in detail in chapter 3).

SURVIVING AN AVALANCHE

Always try to avoid avalanche areas and risk. If you decide to enter an avalanche-prone area, however, make sure you have your avalanche gear with you, and that it is operational. Beacons should have been checked in advance, have new batteries, and turned on to transmit. The AvaLung mouthpiece should be located within inches of your mouth, so that you can quickly insert it if needed. If an avalanche occurs, immediately shout to let everyone else know. Insert the AvaLung mouthpiece, and try to discard gear such as your skis and poles. The exception to discarding gear would be if you can ski to the side and out of danger, or you are wearing items like snowshoes that cannot be quickly taken off. If a safe area is accessible, try to get to it. If you are knocked down, try to stay on top of the surface, using a swimming motion, while heading toward the side of the avalanche. If unable to escape, once the slide begins to slow down, try to get a hand to the surface so it can be seen, and make an air space in front of your face with your other arm. The AvaLung will greatly increase your potential of rescue, and at this point, if you are using one, it's best to relax and conserve your energy.

AVALANCHE RESCUE

Once an avalanche has occurred, the most experienced member of the team should immediately take charge and organize the search. Before doing anything, however, the risk of another avalanche needs to be ruled out, escape routes established, and a lookout assigned. Have all members of the rescue party turn their beacons to the receive mode. If anyone leaves his or her beacon in the transmit mode, you'll waste time tracking this signal. Mark the last position where the victim was seen, and use this as your starting point. Time is crucial. At this point, no one should be sent for help. Every member of the team should stay and search.

SEARCHING WITH AN AVALANCHE RESCUE BEACON

An avalanche rescue has three phases: coarse, fine, and pinpoint. Each phase builds upon the preceding one.

Coarse Search

The coarse search begins by quickly evaluating the snow's surface for partially covered subjects, discarded gear, or terrain features that may predict the person's travel route or resting point. Mark the subject's last known site, along with any other clues, such as found equipment. Trees and rocks are common areas where an individual may become trapped during an avalanche, so probe any that are located in the avalanche's path. This should be a quick, methodical process. Next, starting just above the subject's last known location, line up your team members, spacing them approximately 50 feet apart and facing downhill. Have all members turn their beacon volume all the way up and begin a parallel (to one another) downhill search pattern. Rescuers should rotate the beacons left and right and forward and back as they move. This is necessary due to the wire wrap antenna. A signal can be stronger or weaker based on the rescue beacon's position relative to the subject's beacon. If only one person was caught in the avalanche, once a signal is obtained, two rescuers should begin the fine search process, and all others should get their digging gear ready. If more than one person was involved, one rescuer should begin a fine search and the other members of the rescue team should continue the coarse search; in this situation, turn off the transmitting beacon once a subject is found.

Fine Search using the bracket method

When a signal is picked up, orient the beacon to the strongest signal by rotating it left and right and forward and back. Once the strongest signal is obtained, keep that orientation throughout the search. Walk in a straight line toward the increasing signal, continually reducing the beacon's volume to the lowest audible level. Keeping the beacon oriented, continue your straight line of travel until the signal fades. Mark this spot. Without changing the beacon's orientation, turn around and head back the same way you came. When the signal fades, mark the spot. Move to the center of the bracketed line, turn 90 degrees, and walk in a straight line, reducing the volume as you go. As before, once the signal begins to fade, mark the spot, turn around, and retrace your steps, marking where the signal fades. Keep the beacon

Coarse and fine search for avalanche subject

oriented throughout this process. You now have four fade-out points. Move to the center of this second line, turn 90 degrees, and repeat the process. Continue this process of returning to the center of a line, turning 90 degrees, and marking fade-out points until the distance between these fade-out points is less than 6 feet. You can now move to the pinpoint search.

The cone of silence
A beacon puts out an oval signal that runs up and away on both sides of the antenna, wrapping around the beacon in an oval shape and returning to its base. These centrally connected oval signals create an area called the cone of silence, which is located directly above and below the antenna. If you

move through this area, your signal will drop in intensity while in it but become strong again when you reach the other side. For this reason, when doing the bracket search, you should always go a few feet beyond the signal's weakest point to make sure it doesn't increase again. If it does, then that is the area you should mark. From there, turn around and travel back the same path, marking the spot where the signal transitions from weak to strong. Go to the center of this line and resume your search as done before, marking the line's two lowest signal intensities. The newer dual antenna beacons may make this problem obsolete, but for now, it is still an issue.

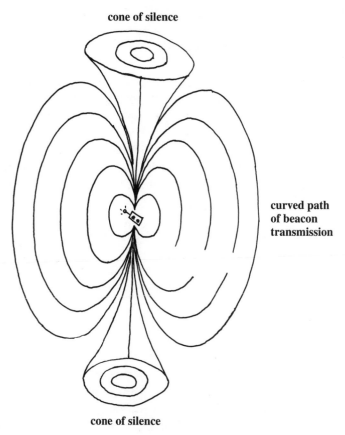

cone of silence

curved path
of beacon
transmission

cone of silence

A beacon signal has a cone of silence.

Fine Search using the Tangential Method

The tangential method is an alternative to the bracket method and is faster when used by someone trained in its method. It is not always successful, however, and should thus be learned as an alternative method and not instead of the bracket method. To use it, orient the beacon to the strongest signal by rotating it left and right and forward and back. Keep this orientation throughout the rescue. Travel toward the strongest signal. If the initial signal drops before you have traveled 15 feet, turn around and go in the opposite direction. After going 15 feet, reorient the beacon to its maximum signal intensity, reduce the volume to the lowest audible level, and move 15 feet, toward the signal's *strongest* intensity. Repeat this process every 15 feet. Since the beacon signal of the subject has a curve (the cone of silence's curve), your search will follow the curve.

Pinpoint Search

With your beacon oriented and close to the snow's surface, begin moving from side to side and front to back, trying to pinpoint the subject's location. During this process, identify the area where the beacon's signal produces its highest intensity while the volume is turned to its lowest level. A lot of beacons actually change tone sound when directly over another one. At this point, begin a quick but gentle probe of the area, taking care not to hurt the subject.

DIGGING OUT AND TREATING THE SUBJECT

Once the subject has been located with the probe, leave it in place as a guide and begin digging. While digging, be careful not to injure the subject. Remove snow from the subject's mouth and assess his or her status. If rescue breathing or CPR is indicated, begin it immediately. Treat for hypothermia and shock, and evaluate for a head or spinal injury.

PROBE SEARCHES

If a rescue beacon is not available, begin a probe search. Taking care not to hurt the subject, gently probe at locations where he or she was last seen, at areas where equipment was found (especially the lowest location), and at likely resting spots. If you don't have a probe, use ski poles or tree branches. After probing likely locations, establish a probe line that starts at the base of the debris and extends up the most likely trajectory.

SURVIVAL TIPS

DON'T TAKE RISKS
Don't be macho and dead! Take the time to evaluate avalanche conditions, and heed the warnings when they are present.

AVOID AVALANCHE AREAS WHENEVER YOU CAN
If you must travel into these areas, learn avalanche safety in advance and practice beacon rescue before you begin each trip.

MAKE SURE YOUR BEACONS WORK
Beacons operate on batteries and are prone to failure from cold soaking and life expectancy. To avoid cold soaking make sure to keep the beacons between your clothing layers. To avoid life expectancy issues, replace batteries before each trip.

13

Health Issues

Survival medicine is simply first aid and CPR with a twist. Ultimately, the environment and the amount of time before you return to civilization may have the biggest impact upon any health issues that arise. The weather may be bad, and the nearest medical facility may be miles from your location. It's highly advisable that you receive adequate first aid and CPR training, and in no way should you consider this chapter a replacement for that instruction.

GENERAL HEALTH ISSUES

Your ability to fend off an injury or infection plays a significant role in how well you will handle any given survival situation. Proper hydration, nutrition, hygiene, and rest all affect your ability to ward off problems encountered in the wilderness.

STAYING HYDRATED

Without water, you'll die in approximately three to five days. In addition, dehydration will directly affect your ability to make logical decisions about how to handle any given problem. Fluids are lost when the body works to warm itself, when sweating or doing intense activity, and when you urinate or defecate. As dehydration starts to set in, you'll begin to have excessive thirst and become irritable, weak, and nauseated. As your symptoms advance, you'll begin having a headache and become dizzy, and eventually your tongue will swell and your vision will be affected. Prevention is the best way to avoid dehydration. This can be accomplished by drinking at least 2 to 3 quarts of water during minimal activity and 4 to 6 quarts during more intense activity. If you should become dehydrated, decrease your activity, get out of the sun, and drink enough potable water to get your urine output up to at least 1 quart in a twenty-four-hour period.

NUTRITION
Nourishing foods increase morale, provide valuable energy, and replace lost nutrients, such as salt, vitamins, and minerals. Food is not as critical as water, and you may be able to go without it for several weeks.

HYGIENE
Not only does staying clean increase morale, but it also helps prevent infection and disease. Methods of staying clean in the wilderness include taking a bath and sun bathing. A sunbath should last from thirty minutes to two hours a day. Keeping your hair trimmed, brushing your teeth and gums, monitoring your feet, and cleaning your cooking utensils after each use are also important tasks that will decrease the risk of illness or infestation.

REST
Providing the body with proper rest helps ensure that you have adequate strength to deal with the stress of initial shock and subsequent trials associated with a survival situation.

TRAUMATIC INJURIES
Traumatic injuries are extremely taxing, and keeping your composure may mean the difference between surviving and not. The treatment of traumatic injuries should therefore follow a logical process. Treat the most life-threatening injuries first: breathing, bleeding, and shock.

AIRWAY, BREATHING, CIRCULATION (ABCs)
To be successful when treating someone whose airway, breathing, or circulation is compromised, you must know CPR. Learn this prior to departing for the wilderness.

BLEEDING (HEMORRHAGE)
There are three types of bleeding. An *arterial bleed* is the most serious of the three and is normally bright red, spurting blood. A *venous bleed* can also be very serious and is usually identified as a steady stream of dark red blood. *Capillary bleeds* are minor, and since the vessels are so close to the skin's surface, the dark red blood typically oozes from the site. Basic treatment options are direct pressure, pressure to pressure points, and rarely, a tourniquet.

Direct pressure

Do not delay in applying pressure, even if you have to use your hand or finger. If materials are available, use a pressure dressing, applied by packing the wound with several sterile dressings, then wrapping it with a continuous bandage. The bandage should be snug, but not so snug as to cut off circulation to the rest of the extremity. To ensure that this doesn't occur, regularly check for pulses and sensations of the extremity beyond the wound site. If blood soaks through the dressing, apply subsequent dressings directly over the first. Leave in place for two days; thereafter, change it daily. If it's an extremity that is bleeding, elevate it above the heart level. In most cases, applying direct pressure for ten minutes will stop the bleeding.

Pressure points

Applying pressure to a blood vessel between the heart and the wound will decrease the amount of blood loss from the injury site. To be effective, this

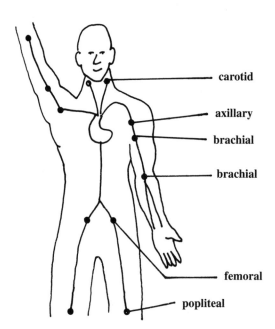

Pressure points can be an effective tool for controlling bleeding.

pressure *must* be applied for about ten minutes. The accompanying diagram shows various pressure points.

Tourniquet

A tourniquet is rarely necessary and should be used only when direct pressure, elevation, and pressure to pressure points have failed, or it's deemed necessary to save a life. The likelihood of losing an extremity from tourniquet use is high; however, once it has been applied, never loosen it. To use a tourniquet, apply a 3- to 4-inch band 2 inches above the wound, so that it is between the wound and the heart. After wrapping the band around the limb several times, tie it into a square knot with a sturdy stick placed in the knot's center, tighten the tourniquet by turning the stick until the blood flow comes to a stop, and secure the stick in place. Mark the victim's head with a big T, and note the time when the tourniquet was applied.

SHOCK

Shock is a direct result of the body's inability to provide a sufficient blood supply to the vital organs. If not treated, it could ultimately lead to death. Signs and symptoms of shock include pale, cold, and clammy skin; a weak, rapid pulse; and feelings of restlessness, disorientation, and faintness. All injuries, no matter how small, can potentially lead to shock, and all victims should be treated as if shock were present. To treat, control the patient's heat loss by covering him or her with any form of dry insulating material, and provide insulation from the ground. If hypothermia is present, treat it. If conscious, lay the victim on his or her back. If unconscious, lay him or her on the side, in case of vomiting. Elevate lower extremities 8 to 12 inches, except when there is a serious head, neck, chest, or abdominal injury. For head or chest injury, raise the victim's upper torso about 15 degrees toward a sitting position.

HEAD INJURIES

Signs and symptoms of a head injury include bleeding, increasing headache, drowsiness, nausea, vomiting, unequal pupils, and unconsciousness. To treat, immobilize the neck if a neck injury is suspected, monitor for any change in mental status, and if conscious, treat the victim for shock by slightly elevating the head and keeping him or her warm. If unconscious, treat the victim for shock by laying him or her on the side to avoid aspiration of vomit.

FRACTURES

Closed fractures

Signs and symptoms of a closed fracture include site deformity, swelling, pain, and an inability to bear weight on the affected extremity. To treat, clean all open wounds, and apply a splint that immobilizes the extremity one joint above and below the fracture site. A splint can be improvised by using strong branches that are held in place with 1-inch-wide bands of clothing or similar material. Once you've applied a splint, monitor for any changes in circulation or sensation. When in doubt about whether something is broken or not, treat it as if it is.

Open fractures

An open fracture has all the signs and symptoms of a closed fracture, with the addition of bone protruding through the skin. Don't push the bone end back in or handle it during the treatment process. To treat, rinse away any dirt and debris with a mixture of 1 quart sterile water and 1 teaspoon salt. After cleaning the bone and the surrounding area, cover the end of the bone with a clean, wet dressing, using the above solution. It's extremely important to prevent the bone ends from drying out. Secure the dressing in place, splint the fracture, and monitor the extremity for any changes in circulation or sensation.

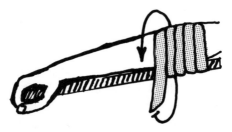

Suspected fractures should be splinted and immobilized.

INJURIES OF JOINTS AND MUSCLES

Sprain
With a sprain, the area of pain is over a joint. Symptoms are similar to those of a closed fracture, and a sprain should be treated as if a fracture exists.

Strain
With a strain, the area of pain is over muscle, not bone. A strain results in localized muscle tenderness, usually as a result of overuse or trauma. To treat, apply moist heat, and discontinue any activity that seems to make it worse.

BURNS
Burns are rated as first, second, or third degree, each indicating increasingly deeper penetration. A first-degree burn causes superficial tissue damage, sparing the underlying skin, and is similar in appearance to a sunburn. A second-degree burn causes damage into the upper portion of the skin, with resultant blister formation that is surrounded by first-degree burn damage. Third-degree burns cause complete destruction of the skin's full thickness and often beyond. In addition, first- and second-degree burns are usually present. To treat burns, cool the skin as rapidly as possible and for at least forty-five minutes. This is extremely important, since many burns continue to cause damage for up to forty-five minutes, even after the heat source has been removed. Remove clothing and jewelry as soon as possible, but don't remove any clothing that is stuck in the burn. Never cover the burn with grease or fats, as they will only increase the risk of infection and are of no value in the treatment process. Clean the burn with sterile (if available) water, apply antibiotic ointment, and cover it with a clean, loose dressing. To avoid infection, leave the bandage in place for six to eight days. After that time, change the bandage as necessary. If the victim is conscious, fluids are a must. Major burns cause a significant amount of fluid loss, and ultimately the victim will go into shock unless these fluids are replaced. If pain medications are available, use them. Burns are extremely painful.

FOREIGN BODIES IN THE EYE

Most eye injuries encountered in the wilderness are a result of dust or dirt blown into the eye by the wind. Symptoms include a red and irritated eye, light sensitivity, and pain. To treat, first look for any foreign bodies that might be causing the irritation. The most common site where dirt or dust can be found is just under the upper eyelid. Invert the lid and try to isolate and remove the irritant. If unable to isolate the cause, rinse the affected eye with clean water for at least ten to fifteen minutes. When rinsing, keep the injured eye lower than the uninjured to ensure that the other eye is not contaminated during the rinsing process. If available, apply ophthalmic antibiotic ointment to the affected eye.

WOUNDS, LACERATIONS, AND INFECTIONS

Clean all wounds, lacerations, and infections, and apply antibiotic ointment, dressing, and a bandage daily.

BLISTERS

Blisters result from the constant rubbing of your skin against a sock or boot. The best treatment is prevention. Monitor your feet for hot spots or areas that become red and inflamed. If you develop a hot spot, apply a wide band of adhesive tape across and well beyond the affected area. If you have tincture of benzoin, use it. It'll make the tape adhere better, and it also helps toughen the skin. To treat a blister, cut a blister-size hole in the center of a piece of moleskin, and place it so that the hole is directly over the blister. This will take the pressure off the blister and place it on the surrounding moleskin. Try to avoid popping the blister; if it does break open, treat it as an open wound by applying antibiotic ointment and a bandage.

THORNS AND SPLINTERS

Remove any thorns and splinters, and to prevent infection, apply antibiotic ointment, dressing, and a bandage.

ENVIRONMENTAL INJURIES AND ILLNESSES

The environment challenges us in many different ways, and it needs to be respected. Realize that it cannot be conquered. Adapting and being properly prepared will play a significant role in surviving nature's sometimes awesome power.

COLD INJURIES

Hypothermia

Hypothermia refers to an abnormally low body temperature. Symptoms include uncontrollable shivering, slurred speech, abnormal behavior, fatigue and drowsiness, decreased hand and body coordination, and weakened respiration and pulse. Body heat may have been lost through radiation, conduction, evaporation, convection, and/or respiration. The best treatment is prevention through avoidance of exposure and early recognition. Dressing appropriately for the environment and maintaining adequate hydration can help you avoid most problems with hypothermia. If hypothermia does occur, it should be treated without delay. Begin treatment by stopping continued heat loss. Get out of the wind and moisture, and put on dry clothes, a hat, and gloves. If you have a sleeping bag, take off your clothes, fluff the bag, and climb inside. In an extreme case, someone else should disrobe and climb inside the bag with the victim. If conscious, the victim should consume warm fluids and carbohydrates.

Frostbite

Frostbite commonly affects toes, fingers, and face. The best treatment is prevention. Using the COLDER acronym (see chapter 4) and understanding how heat is lost are two methods of ensuring that frostbite doesn't occur. There are two types of frostbite: superficial or deep. *Superficial frostbite* causes cold, numb, and painful extremities that appear white or grayish in color. To treat, rewarm the affected part with your own or someone else's body heat: hands should be placed in the armpits, feet on another person's abdomen. Cover other exposed areas with loose, layered material. Never blow on your hands; the resultant moisture will cause the skin to freeze or refreeze. *Deep frostbite* causes your skin to take on a white appearance, lose feeling, and become extremely hard. Should you sustain a deep frostbite injury, don't attempt to rewarm it. Rewarming it will be extremely painful, and a rewarmed frostbitten limb will be rendered useless, whereas you can walk on a frostbitten limb. Prevent any additional freezing and injury from occurring by wearing proper clothing and avoiding further exposure to the elements.

Immersion injuries

Trench foot is a direct result of long-term exposure of the feet to cold, wet socks. A similar condition can affect the hands. It usually takes several days to weeks of this exposure before the damage occurs. Symptoms include painful, swollen feet, or hands that have a waterlogged appearance. Since immersion injuries can be so debilitating, it's best to prevent them altogether by changing wet socks or gloves quickly, not wearing tight clothing, and increasing foot circulation with regular massages. If an immersion injury develops, treat it by keeping the hands and feet dry and elevated. Since rubbing may result in further tissue damage, pat wet areas dry.

Snow blindness

Snow blindness is a result of exposure of the eyes to the sun's ultraviolet rays. It most often occurs in areas where sunlight is reflected off the snow or light-colored rocks. The resultant burn to the eyes' surface can be quite debilitating. Symptoms include bloodshot and tearing eyes, a painful and gritty sensation in the eyes, light sensitivity, and headaches. Prevention by wearing 100 percent UV sunglasses is a must. If snow blindness does occur, avoid further exposure, apply a cool wet compress to the eyes, and treat the pain with aspirin, as needed. If symptoms are severe, apply an eye patch for twenty-four to forty-eight hours.

HEAT INJURIES

Sunburn

Prevent sunburn by using a strong sunscreen whenever necessary. If a burn should occur, apply cool compresses, avoid further exposure, and cover any areas that have been or may become burned.

Muscle cramps

Muscle cramps may result from excessive salt loss from the body, exposure to a hot climate, or excessive sweating. Painful muscle cramps usually occur in the calf or abdomen, while the victim's body temperature is normal. To treat, immediately stretch the affected muscle. The best way to prevent recurrence is to drink 2 to 3 quarts of water per day with minimal activity, or 4 to 6 quarts per day when in cold or hot environments or during heavy activity.

Heat exhaustion

Heat exhaustion is a result of physical activity in a hot environment and is usually accompanied by some component of dehydration. Symptoms include feeling faint or weak, cold and clammy skin, headache, nausea, and confusion. To treat, rest in a cool, shady area and drink plenty of water. Since heat exhaustion is a form of shock, the victim should lie down and elevate the feet 8 to 12 inches.

Heatstroke

Heatstroke occurs when the body is unable to adequately lose its heat. As a result, body temperature rises to such high levels that damage to the brain and vital organs occur. Symptoms include flushed dry skin, headache, weakness, lightheadedness, rapid full pulse, confusion, and in severe cases, unconsciousness and convulsions. Heatstroke is a true emergency and should be avoided at all costs. Immediate treatment is imperative. Cool the victim by removing his or her clothing and covering the body with wet towels or submerging it in water that is cool but not icy. Fanning is also helpful. Be careful to avoid cooling to the point of hypothermia.

ALTITUDE ILLNESSES

As your elevation increases, so does your risk of developing a form of altitude illness. As a general rule, most mountaineers use the following three levels of altitude to determine their potential for medical problems: high altitude, 8,000 to 14,000 feet; very high altitude, 14,000 to 18,000 feet; extreme high altitude, 18,000 feet and above. Since most travelers seldom venture to heights greater than 14,000 feet, the majority of altitude illnesses are seen in the high-altitude range.

As your altitude increases, your body goes through compensatory changes, which include increased respiratory and heart rates, increased red blood cell and capillary production and changes in the body's oxygen delivery capacity. Most of these changes occur within several days to weeks of exposure at high altitudes. To diminish the effects of altitude, do a gradual ascent, avoid heavy exertion for several days after rapidly ascending to high altitudes, and ingest only small amounts of salt. If you have a history of pulmonary edema or worse, consider taking Diamox (acetazolamide), a prescription medication that is contraindicated for individuals with kidney, eye, or liver disease. The usual dose is 250 milligrams, taken two to four times a day. It's started twenty-four to forty-eight hours prior to ascent and continued, while at high altitude, for forty-eight hours or as long as needed.

High-altitude illnesses are a direct result of a reduction in the body's oxygen supply. This reduction occurs in response to the decreased atmospheric pressure associated with higher elevations. The three illnesses of high altitude are acute mountain sickness, high-altitude pulmonary edema, and high-altitude cerebral edema.

Acute mountain sickness

Acute mountain sickness usually occurs as a result of decreased oxygen supply to the brain at altitudes greater than 8,000 feet. Symptoms include headache, fatigue, dizziness, shortness of breath, decreased appetite, nausea and vomiting, feelings of uneasiness, cyanosis (bluing around lips and fingers), and fluid retention in face and hands. In severe cases, there may be evidence of some impaired mental function, such as forgetfulness, loss of memory, decreased coordination, hallucinations, or even psychotic behavior. To prevent, allow time to acclimatize by keeping activity to a minimum for the first two to three days after arriving at elevations greater than 8,000 feet; avoid alcohol and tobacco; eat small, high-carbohydrate meals; and drink plenty of fluids. If symptoms are severe and oxygen is available, give 2 liters per minute through a face mask for a minimum of fifteen minutes. If symptoms persist or worsen, descend at least 2,000 to 3,000 feet; this is usually enough to relieve symptoms.

High-altitude pulmonary edema (HAPE)

High-altitude pulmonary edema is an extremely common and dangerous type of altitude illness that results from abnormal accumulation of fluid in the lungs. It most often occurs when a climber rapidly ascends above 8,000 feet and, instead of resting for several days, immediately begins performing strenuous activities. Symptoms include signs of acute mountain sickness, shortness of breath with exertion that may progress to shortness of breath at rest as time goes by, shortness of breath when lying down (this symptom usually makes it difficult for the victim to sleep), and a dry cough that, in time, will progress to a wet, productive, and persistent cough. If symptoms progress, the climber may show symptoms of impaired mental function similar to those seen in acute mountain sickness. If the climber becomes unconscious, death will occur within several hours unless a quick descent is made and oxygen treatment started. An early diagnosis is the key to successfully treating pulmonary edema. Once identified, immediately descend a minimum of 2,000 to 3,000 feet, or until symptoms begin to improve. Once down, rest for two to three days, and allow the fluid that has accumulated in the lungs to be reabsorbed by the body. If oxygen is available, administer it, via a tight-fitting face mask, at 4 to 6 liters per minute for fifteen minutes, and then decrease its flow rate to 2 liters per minute. Continue using the oxygen for an additional twelve hours if possible. If the victim has moderate to severe HAPE, he or she should be evacuated to the nearest hospital as soon as possible. If prone to HAPE, it may be worth trying Diamox prior to the climb (see above).

High-altitude cerebral edema (HACE)

High-altitude cerebral edema is swelling of the brain, and it most often occurs at altitudes greater than 12,000 feet. The edema forms as a consequence of the body's decreased supply of oxygen, a condition known as hypoxia. Symptoms include signs of acute mountain sickness, headache that is usually severe and unrelenting, abnormal mental function (such as confusion, loss of memory, poor judgment, or hallucinations), and ataxia (poor coordination). An extreme case can result in coma or death. Early recognition is of the utmost importance in saving someone who develops HACE. A person with a severe chronic headache with confusion and/or ataxia must be treated for high-altitude cerebral edema—a true emergency. To treat, descend immediately. If the victim is ataxic or confused, he or she will need help. If oxygen is available, administer it as described above for a HAPE victim. Even if the victim recovers, he or she shouldn't return to the climb. If a person becomes unconscious or has severe symptoms, all efforts should be made for an air evacuation to the nearest hospital.

INSECT BITES AND STINGS

Ticks

To remove a tick, grasp it at the base of its body, where its mouth attaches to the skin, and apply gentle backward pressure until it releases its hold. If its head isn't removed, treat as any other open wound, applying antibiotic ointment and a bandage.

Bee or wasps

If stung by a bee or wasp, immediately remove the stinger by scraping the skin, at a 90-degree angle, with a knife or your fingernail. This will decrease the amount of venom that is absorbed into the skin. Applying cold compresses and/or a cool paste made of mud or ashes will help relieve the pain and itching. To avoid infection, don't scratch the stinger site. If carrying a bee sting kit, review the procedures of its use prior to departing for the wilderness. If someone has an allergic anaphylactic reaction, it will be necessary to act fast. Using the medications in the bee sting kit and following basic first-aid principles will, in most cases, reverse the symptoms associated with this type of reaction.

Mosquitoes

Use insect repellent and/or cover the body's exposed parts with clothing or mud to decrease the number of bites you'll experience from these pesky insects.

SURVIVAL STRESS

The effects of stress in a survival situation cannot be understated. To decrease its magnitude, you must not only understand it, but also prevail over it. The environment, your condition, and the availability of materials will either raise or decrease the amount of stress you'll experience. The most important key to overcoming survival stresses is the survivor's will. The will or drive to survive is not something that can be taught. However, your will is directly affected by the amount of stress associated with a survival situation. Observing the six Ps of survival—proper prior preparation prevents poor performance—will help alleviate some of this stress. In addition, my three-step approach to survival—keeping a clear head and thinking logically, prioritizing your needs, and improvising—will help raise your comfort level.

SURVIVAL TIPS

TAKE CARE OF YOUR *FIVE SURVIVAL ESSENTIALS* AND HEALTH NEEDS SHOULD NOT BE AN ISSUE.

For example, properly meeting your personal protection needs will decrease the odds of environmental injuries (cold and hot injuries). In addition, using the *three step approach* to survival will decrease the effects of psychological stress and make you feel more confident about your outcome.

MOTIVATION CAN BE OBTAINED IN MANY WAYS.

Faith, fear, and pride are three examples of what people have used to overcome what appeared to be insurmountable. Several years back I met a man who told me that his sole motivation for rescue was that his wife had the checkbook. Although I can't verify the validity of his story I did find it amusing. What motivates you? Whatever it is you'll need to learn to harness it and allow it to produce the energy needed to overcome your preconceived limits.

14

Animals

POLAR BEARS

DESCRIPTION

Polar bears are large, white, four-footed carnivores (meat eaters) that range in size from 350 to 1,100 pounds. The adult male is larger (8 to 11 feet long) and appears leaner than the smaller, stocky female (6 to 8 feet long). In addition, the male has a longer neck and higher rump than the female. These bears can be found in Alaska, Canada, Russia, Greenland, and Norway. Polar bears are very nomadic and can be seen on pack ice, coastal islands, coastlines, and even out in arctic waters. Around November, pregnant female polar bears dig dens and hibernate, emerging in late March or early April with their newborn cubs.

Polar bear

WHAT YOU SHOULD KNOW
As a carnivore, a polar bear's primary diet consists of seals, but when hungry, they have been known to prey on humans. They have an acute sense of smell, so when you're in polar bear country, make every effort to eliminate or reduce odors on yourself and in your camp.

BEFORE YOU GO
The best advice I can give is to avoid polar bear country. If you intend to travel in one of these areas, however, ask park or forest rangers about possible bear activity in the area where you are headed, and take time to research seasonal bear sightings there. If you are unfamiliar with an area or information is scarce, you should consider hiring a local guide.

ONCE YOU GO
Always be on the lookout for polar bears, and avoid traveling when visibility is poor. Avoiding areas where polar bears concentrate can reduce the potential for aggressive interaction. These areas include boulders, pressure ridges, coastlines, icebergs, islets just offshore, maternal den sites, summer retreats, and fall staging sites where bears congregate to wait for ice to form. Since polar bears are curious creatures with an acute sense of smell, keep food and garbage in bearproof containers, and stay away from carcasses. Menstruating females should use tampons instead of pads, placing used ones in a bearproof garbage container. Since polar bears rarely do a bluff charge, a rapidly approaching bear should be interpreted as aggression that will end in physical contact. With this in mind, protect your camp by using a warning system, trained alert dogs, or both to warn of a polar bear's approach. If a bear is spotted, go immediately to a safe and secure location, like a building. If this is not possible, deterrents like pepper spray and loud noises are sometimes helpful, as long as you know how to use them. If a polar bear attacks, use any weapon to try to dissuade it from continuing its aggressive behavior.

BROWN BEARS

DESCRIPTION
Brown bears, called grizzlies in the Lower 48, are four-footed omnivores, meaning they eat both vegetation and animals. They range in size from

Brown bear

300 to 850 pounds, with an average height of 3.5 to 4 feet at the shoulder when on all four legs, and 6 to 7 feet when standing upright. Its distinctive shoulder hump, color, and long snout distinguish the brown bear from other bears. These bears can be found in Alaska, Wyoming, Montana, Idaho, and Washington, as well as Canada, eastern and western Europe, northern Asia, and Japan. The brown bear lives in a variety of environments that include dense forests, subalpine meadows, and arctic tundra. The brown bear's diet varies greatly; it has been known to eat grasses, sedges, roots, berries, insects, fish, carrion, and small and large mammals. Brown bears hibernate during winter months, until April or May, usually five to eight months.

WHAT YOU SHOULD KNOW
Contrary to popular legend, encounters with grizzly bears are infrequent, and grizzlies do not naturally behave aggressively toward humans. As solitary animals, these bears actually try to avoid contact with other bears and people. The rare grizzly attack occurs when the bear has been surprised, it feels the need to protect its cubs or food, it is sick or wounded, or a human is acting in an aggressive fashion. The importance of keeping grizzlies out of

human food and garbage cannot be stressed enough. Once a bear becomes accustomed to these food sources, it will lose its natural fear of close contact with humans. The brown bear uses its acute sense of smell, keen eyesight, and excellent hearing to stay abreast of its surroundings and can often be seen standing on its hind legs to obtain more information from these senses. A grizzly bear can run and climb a tree faster than you can.

BEFORE YOU GO
Talk to park or forest rangers about possible bear activity in the area where you are headed, and take time to research seasonal bear sightings there. Let someone know where you are going and when you plan to return.

ONCE YOU GO
To avoid sudden encounters, stay on well-established trails, be aware of your surroundings, and make noise by occasionally yelling, clapping, or wearing a bear bell. Watch for bear signs like tracks, scat, torn-up logs, and turned-over rocks. If you have children with you, keep them close by. Do not let them wander off-trail and into the wilderness. Since bears have an acute sense of smell, always cook away from your campsite, and sleep in different clothes than those you cooked in. Should you encounter a grizzly bear, stay calm, and determine the potential risk before deciding what to do. A calm, curious bear often stands on its hind legs, sniffing the air. If a bear is looking in your direction, avoid direct eye contact, speak in a soft monotone, and slowly back away. Never turn your back and run, as this may precipitate a bear attack. Before backing away, if you have a hat or bandanna (a good thing to have when in bear country), drop it on the ground. An approaching bear will often stop to sniff the object, which gives you more time to distance yourself from it. If a bear charges, stand your ground. Bears often "bluff charge" several times before leaving. If the bear is not bluffing and makes contact with you, play dead by curling into a ball or lying flat, while covering your neck with your hands and arms. Since your backpack adds protection, leave it on. During the attack, stay facedown, and don't move or make a sound until the bear is gone. When prepared in advance and used correctly, a deterrent like bear pepper spray can be effective at repelling an approaching bear.

BLACK BEARS

DESCRIPTION

Black bears are four-footed omnivores, eating both vegetation and animals. They range in size from 100 to 300 pounds. In addition to being smaller than the brown bear, black bears do not have a shoulder hump, and their snout is shorter and less pointed. American black bears are found in thirty-two states, as well as Mexico and Canada. Black bears are primarily found in forested areas, including the tundra, and wetlands. The bear's diet primarily consists of nuts and berries but can also include other plants, insects, small mammals, carrion, salmon, and an occasional young deer or moose calf. Most black bears hibernate during the winter months. In areas of warmer weather and an available food supply, however, black bears have been known not to hibernate at all. Like the grizzly, a black bear can run and climb a tree faster than you can.

WHAT YOU SHOULD KNOW

Encounters with black bears are infrequent, and black bears do not naturally behave aggressively toward humans. As solitary animals, these bears actually try to avoid contact with other bears and people. The rare attack occurs when the bear has been surprised, it feels the need to protect its cubs or food, it is sick or wounded, or a human is acting in an aggressive fashion.

Black bear

ONCE YOU GO

Black bears are rarely a threat to the backcountry traveler, since they often turn and run away when startled by a human. Should a black bear attack, however, deterrents like pepper spray and loud noises are sometimes helpful, as long as you know how to use them. If deterrents don't work and an attack appears imminent, use any weapon to try to dissuade the bear from continuing its aggressive behavior.

PUMAS

DESCRIPTION

The puma is also known as cougar, mountain lion, panther, and catamount. Pumas average 3.5 to 5.5 feet in length and can weigh up to 225 pounds. They are found throughout the Western Hemisphere, from Canada to Argentina, residing in coniferous forests, swamps, grasslands, and tropical forests. The puma's diet primarily consists of large mammals, such as deer, but they have also been known to eat smaller game, including beavers, rabbits, squirrels, and mice.

WHAT YOU SHOULD KNOW

Encounters with pumas are infrequent, and pumas do not naturally behave aggressively toward humans. As solitary animals, these cats actually try to avoid contact with other cats and people. The rare puma attack occurs

Puma

when the cat has been surprised, it feels the need to protect its cubs or food, it is sick or wounded, or a human is acting in an aggressive fashion.

BEFORE YOU GO
Talk to park or forest rangers about possible puma activity in the area where you are headed, and take time to research seasonal puma sightings there. Let someone know where you are going and when you plan to return.

ONCE YOU GO
To avoid sudden encounters, stay on well-established trails, be aware of your surroundings, and avoid hiking alone or at dawn and dusk, when pumas are most active. If you have children with you, keep them close by. Do not let them wander off-trail or into the wilderness. Should you encounter a puma, stay calm, and try to make yourself appear bigger by opening your coat or standing close to another person while slowly backing away. If the cat continues to act in an aggressive manner, throw stones or sticks at it. Should it attack, protect your neck, and aggressively fight back using anything at your disposal.

GRAY WOLVES

DESCRIPTION
The gray wolf is a four-footed carnivore that ranges in size from 55 to 150 pounds and stands approximately 26 to 32 inches at the shoulder. Gray wolves are found in Alaska, Idaho, Michigan, Minnesota, Montana, Wisconsin, and Wyoming, as well as Canada, Europe, Asia, the Middle East, and Russia. They are primarily located in forests, tundra, deserts, plains, and mountains. The wolf's diet mainly consists of large, hoofed mammals, such as deer and elk, though on occasion they also prey on smaller animals, such as beavers or rabbits.

WHAT YOU SHOULD KNOW
Encounters with wolves are infrequent, and wolves do not naturally behave aggressively toward humans. Wolves live in packs, which include a dominant alpha male and female, along with their offspring, and they communicate by scent marking, vocalizing, facial expressions, and body postures.

Gray Wolf

ONCE YOU GO
To avoid sudden encounters, stay on well-established trails, be aware of your surroundings, and avoid hiking alone or at dawn and dusk, when wolves are most active. If you have children with you, keep them close by. Do not let them wander off-trail or into the wilderness. Wolves are generally shy and timid, and the likelihood of an attack is extremely remote.

MOOSE

DESCRIPTION
Moose are four-footed vegetarians that can weigh as much as 1,600 pounds and stand as tall as 6.5 feet at the shoulder. They are found in the northern United States, Canada, Europe, and Asia, usually in forested areas. A moose's diet primarily consists of new tree growth (aspen, poplar, willow, birch, dogwood, and balsam fir) and underwater vegetation. Although moose can run fast, a large percentage of yearlings fall prey to wolves and bears.

WHAT YOU SHOULD KNOW
Moose are generally solitary animals and are not normally aggressive toward humans. The rare moose attack occurs during mating season, when the animal believes its calf or food is threatened, it is tired of walking in deep snow, or it is being harassed by people.

ONCE YOU GO
To avoid sudden encounters, stay on well-established trails, and be aware of your surroundings. Should you encounter a moose and it begins walking toward you, stay calm, back away, and look for a tree or other object to put between you and the animal. Like brown bears, moose will often do a bluff

Moose

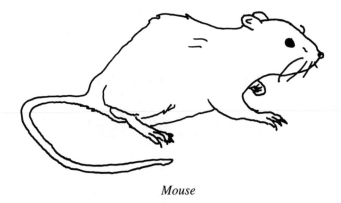

Mouse

charge. Unlike your behavior with the bear, however, you should run and look for a tree or other obstacle to get between you and a charging moose. If a moose should knock you down, curl up into a fetal position, and use your arms and hands to protect your neck and head. Do not move until the moose has left and is a safe distance away from you.

SURVIVAL TIP

MICE
Although mice are not normally considered a deadly problem for the back-country traveler, they can cause a lot of damage. They will chew through tents and gear in an attempt to access food. To avoid attracting mice, cook away from your campsite, sleep in different clothes than those you cooked in, and store all food inside a well-protected food cache.

Survival and First-Aid Kits

Obtaining prior knowledge and skill in the basic elements of survival is the key to ensuring a safe wilderness experience. In addition, proper preparation will prevent poor performance in almost any survival setting and will ultimately reduce the amount of stress you might experience. Central to your preparation are adequate survival and first-aid kits. These kits will play an instrumental role in how you meet your needs. Below are listed suggested items for these two kits.

SURVIVAL KIT

- Map
- Compass
- Flashlight
- Matches and waterproof container
- Fire starter
- Extra food
- Pocketknife
- Extra clothing
- Signal mirror
- Whistle
- Metal cup
- Water bottle
- Plastic bag
- Copper wire
- Fishing line and hooks
- Nonlubricated condoms for water storage
- Sunglasses and sunscreen

FIRST-AID KIT

- Aspirin
- Water purification tablets
- Scissors
- Sunscreen
- Routine medications
- Matches
- Band-Aids
- Emergency blanket
- Antihistamine
- Tincture of benzoin
- Roll of gauze
- Medical tape
- Triangular bandage
- Tweezers
- Moleskin
- Various dressings
- Chapstick
- Soap
- Antibiotic ointment
- Snakebite kit
- Bee sting kit

Knots and Lashes

SQUARE KNOT

The square knot connects two ropes of equal diameter.

DOUBLE SHEET BEND

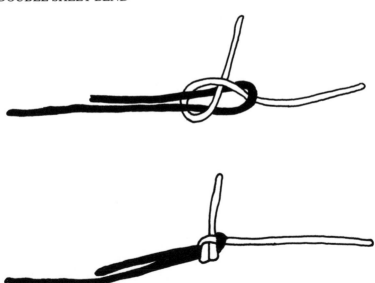

The double sheet bend connects two ropes of different diameter.

OVERHAND FIXED LOOP

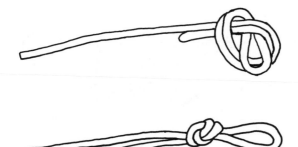

The overhand fixed loop has multiple uses in a survival setting.

BOWLINE

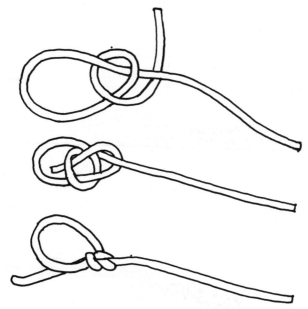

Unlike the overhand fixed loop, the bowline is much easier to untie after you use it.

DOUBLE HALF HITCH

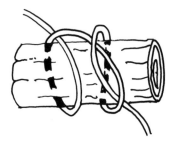

The double half hitch secures a line to a stationary object.

SQUARE LASH

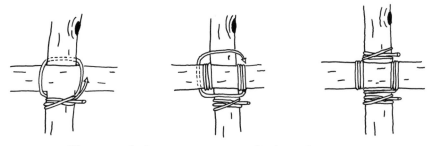

The square lash secures two perpendicular poles together.

SHEAR LASH

The shear lash attaches several parallel poles together.

Index